Journey *to*
SIGNIFICANCE

Navigating Roadblocks - Celebrating Milestones

Greg White

WESTBOW
P R E S S®
A DIVISION OF THOMAS NELSON
& ZONDERVAN

WestBow Press books may be ordered through booksellers or by contacting:

WestBow Press
A Division of Thomas Nelson & Zondervan
1663 Liberty Drive
Bloomington, IN 47403
www.westbowpress.com
844-714-3454

ISBN: 978-1-6642-3181-8 (sc)
ISBN: 978-1-6642-3182-5 (hc)
ISBN: 978-1-6642-3180-1 (e)

Library of Congress Control Number: 2021908138

Print information available on the last page.

WestBow Press rev. date: 04/27/2021

Dedication

This book is dedicated to my father, Cecil "Pete" White, who lived a life of significance. And to my father-in-law, Norman Lanz, who encouraged me. Your lives live on in the men you touched with your example and encouragment.

Foreword

Lost in the Alps! It's a horrible feeling. As a young teenager, I had a "Once in a lifetime" opportunity to attend a national young conference in Switzerland. The conference included a mountain climbing experience. Each group had a guide and they explained the path. A group of ten students, myself included, just headed up the mountain. Imagine our emotions when the path we were on came to a sudden and abrupt end. We hadn't seen another student or group for a couple of hours. We were lost, alone and confused. Heading across the face of the mountain, we came across another group in the late afternoon. We traveled with them for the next hour and listened with amazement as the guide explained the history and beauty of the mountain. Their guide was an expert who had lived on the mountain all of her life. She had travelled the paths, worked around the tough places and celebrated the history of her journey.

We were not only physically lost but imagine the five or six hours of incredible information that we had missed. We rode a cable car down the mountain that evening. The other students were abuzz with the stories of their day as we sat in discouragement at our loss.

Too many people find themselves frustrated by the roadblocks of life! In our frustration, we lose the opportunity to celebrate the milestones that we pass. Don't look back someday at the end of your "once in a lifetime" journey and be filled with loss. You should be able to look back with celebration! The lesson is easy. Don't go the journey alone!

Greg White is a valuable guide! He has walked the paths of life, time and time again. Journey to significance is filled with experiential wisdom and practical steps to help you navigate roadblocks and celebrate the milestones! I love these nuggets from Greg's book. "Significance is a day-to-day expedition, not a destination!" and "Face your doubts...... Face the Truth!... Allow truth to redesign your map!"

Phil Schneider
Superintendent
Illinois District Council
Assemblies of God

After years as a successful pastor Greg White discovered a great passion in the area of leadership. He was not only a wonderful leader, but also a student and then a teacher in principles of leadership. As you make your way on the journey through these pages you will be introduced to leadership concepts that have become an integral part of Greg's life. You'll be challenged to "up your game." Pages in any book may convey ideas and information but it's more difficult, at times, to catch the spirit of a person. I pray you'll catch his spirit. But....you won't be able to hear his contagious laughter. Yet I encourage you to pull up a chair, pour a cup of coffee and crack open his effort to pass along hard earned lessons on an often overlooked topic. And maybe...just maybe, you'll even hear an echo of his soft voice and feel a bit of a hug from his pastoral heart.

Dr. Tim Stearman
Church of the Nazarene

Introduction

How many remember your time in grade school? What kind of impact did those days have on your life? I clearly remember one day while I was sitting in class in the sixth grade. I was not paying attention (I am ADHD), I was looking out the window instead of at the teacher. I was dreaming about the future, wondering what kind of person I would be, what I was going to do with my life. My teacher, Mrs. Webb, called my name out and added, "I want to see you after class." My heart beat faster, my face flushed, and all the other kids in class looked at me with big smiles. After class I walked slowly toward Mrs.Webb's desk and stood there looking at my teacher, wondering what kind of trouble I was going to be in. She looked up at me and said, "I notice you daydreaming during class time." I said, "yes, ma'am." She then said something that to this day still surprises me, "Greg, don't let anyone steal your dreams." I walked home by myself thinking about what she had placed in my life, encouragement to dream; encouragement to think far into the future. I can't explain the impact this had on my life at at early age. She added value to me. She showed me I was valuable, and my dreams were valuable enough to contemplate and guard. This was one of the times I remember someone demonstrating significance.

What does significance mean to you?

When you strive for significance, what are you striving for?

What is keeping you from feeling significant?

On Jackie Robinson's gravestone is one of his most famous quotes, "A life isn't important except for its impact on others' lives."[1]

John Maxwell writes in his book, *Intentional Living*, "To be significant, all you have to do is make a difference with others wherever you are, with whatever you have, day by day."[2]

Here is the question: What or who did I make better today?

Significance is not about you. It is about other people—improving or adding value to their lives. It is about improving your church or business.

When Nancy and I began ministry, pastoring our first church, one of the goals we set was to leave a church better than when we came. I was taught that when setting goals, one qualification is for goals to be realistic. Setting a goal to leave a place better than one found it is a realistic goal, especially if the church or business is on a downhill spiral and some people believe it should be shut down. However, leaving some places better than you found them may not be so realistic or easy. In fact, it may seem frightening. Yet any goal you set in life that does not challenge you will not inspire you to move forward.

▲ REFLECTION

Which of your goals are challenging you today?

Which goals are on the back burner because they do not inspire you?

What are different ways you can make a positive difference in the lives of others today?

What kind of difference do you want to make?

Nelson Mandela, speaking at a ninetieth birthday celebration, said, "What counts in life is not the mere fact that we have lived. It is what difference we have made in the lives of others that will determine the significance of the life we lead."[3]

To make an impact on the lives of others, you must be willing to overcome roadblocks you face in your journey to significance.

And it shall be said, "Build up, build up, prepare the way, remove every obstruction from my people's way" (Isa 57:14).

Significance is a day-to-day expedition, not a destination.

CHAPTER 1

Preparing for the Journey

MILESTONE: COMPASSION

Jesse Owens at times used this phrase, "The battles that count aren't the ones for gold medals. The struggles within yourselves, the invisible, the inevitable battles inside of us all, that's where it's at."[4]

The roadblocks within are the most challenging to maneuver. The battle rages when you are alone and provokes you when you are with others.

To ignore these battles—these roadblocks in your path—will destroy your hopes and dreams, and undermine your goals for the future. You cannot go forward in life without facing roadblocks and fighting battles to overcome them. Each roadblock you face takes physical, mental, emotional, and spiritual energy.

As you overcome one roadblock, you must rest, renew, and rejoice. As you celebrate, you find energy for dealing with the next one in your path.

▲ ROADBLOCK

An obstacle is defined as something that blocks one's way so movement or progress is prevented or made more difficult. Other words for *obstacle* are *barrier, hurdle, stumbling block, impediment, hindrance, complication,* and *difficulty.* Roadblock is another colloquial word used for an obstacle faced in the journey through life. Have you noticed when you come to a roadblock there is an alternate route, sometimes for miles till you get back on the road you were traveling to get to your destination. Roadblocks come in our lives and we must navigate wisely to get back on course.

Booker T. Washington wrote in his autobiography, *Up from Slavery*, "I have learned that success is to be measured not so much by the position that one has reached in life as by the obstacles which he has had to overcome while trying to succeed."[5]

Everyone faces roadblocks! They come in many forms, sizes, and degrees of difficulty.

▲ REFLECTION

What are roadblocks you face as you try to have a positive impact on your church, your business, or people with whom you live and work?

Various ways can be found to overcome roadblocks. The real concern is finding victory navigating to overcoming the roadblocks that appear in your path and keep you from moving forward.

The first roadblock you must navigate and perhaps the most difficult to maneuver, is selfishness. A person who is selfish cares only for hisself or herself.

The Apostle John provides a personal example of an roadblock he faced in one church in 3 John 1:9–10.

> I have written something to the church, but Diotrephes, who likes to put himself first, does not acknowledge our authority. So if I come, I will bring up whatever he is doing, talking wicked nonsense against us. And not content with that, he refuses to welcome the brothers.

John had just written earlier in verse 4, "I have no greater joy than to hear that my children are walking in the truth." Then he admonishes believers to walk in truth by doing good, drawing attention to the positive example of Demetrius.

> "Beloved, do not imitate evil but imitate good. Whoever does good is from God; whoever does evil has not seen God. Demetrius has received a good testimony from everyone, and from the truth itself" (vv. 11–12).

◭ REFLECTION

Which one describes you: Diotrephes or Demetrius?
Which attitude do you move toward naturally?
When do you feel stuck between the two?
Selfishness damages relationships, breeds unhealthy relationships and will eventually destroy any connection with healthy people.
The realm of self (selfishness) is illustrated by putting a circle around your feet.[6] The larger the circle—the more selfish you are—the more you push healthy relationships away. And unhealthy people step into your drama, adding their drama. The smaller the circle, the deeper your connections with healthy people.
Your responsibility is to keep the circle small, to keep yourself healthy. The first person you must keep healthy is yourself; lead yourself first.

◭ OVERCOMING ROADBLOCKS

Before you can meet the first milestone to significance in your leadership journey, you must address personal roadblocks blocking you. To minister, lead, and serve people, you need to decrease the circle of the realm of self and live in the realm of being unselfish. You do this by focusing on the needs of others. You must move from being egocentric to being *other-centric*. You must come face-to-face with the decision Jesus asks of you to deny yourself, take up your cross, and follow Him (Matt 16:24).

The cross represents all Jesus has done by His sacrificial death. He died that you might have life.

You must take up your cross. One way to look at it is that your cross represents dying to self. (A man on a cross knows his life is ending.) Denying self calls for absolute surrender. Denying self and taking up one's cross daily is moving from Jesus being resident in one's life to Jesus being King of one's life. It requires turning from selfishness to servanthood.

The new path is different from the old path of sin you left behind. As you accept the weight of the cross on your shoulders, you let go of the past. Releasing the pull of the flesh (the old man) frees you to move forward to follow Jesus and take on His character.

In the past, I loved to go climbing in the Rocky Mountains. The feel of the pressure of the climbing harness around my waist with a rope attached and in place freed me to focus on the climb. Feeling the weight of the cross on my shoulders keeps my focus on denying self and following Jesus.

I grew up in Russel Heights in the city of Russel, Kentucky. Going to school was a downhill walk, but going home was uphill. Some would say it is not an easy road to walk, but I knew when I got home that dinner was being prepared. In the winter, we would sleigh ride from the top to the bottom of the hill, almost one mile. Yet, we knew if we wanted to ride the sled again, we had to walk to the top of the hill. Riding down was thrilling and fun, but walking up the hill was work. We learned that if we wanted the thrill of the ride, we had to walk to the top of the hill.

If achievement in life is like a sleigh ride down a hill as a child, the lesson is that one must face the climb uphill to have success.

Principles for navigating roadblocks include the following:

• You must give up to take up.
• The road to success is uphill.

Conquering Milestone: Compassion (Love)

In the Old Testament, the Ten Commandments are like stop signs or red lights. They tell you what not to do. The Great Commandment in the New Testament is a green light, and it is always green. Pursue it enthusiastically! The Great Commandment is written in the positive, "You shall love the Lord your God." Circle the word "your." This commandment is very personal. He is your God. This relationship is very personal!

At times, you find it difficult to walk strong in your relationship with God. In those times, you are usually struggling within. It is not the storm on the outside that affects as much as the undercurrent on the inside.

You need to keep your relationship with Jesus close! When you set a priority on this relationship, all other priorities fall into place.

The Greek philosopher Pittacus says, "Hard it is to be good."[7] I believe if Pittacus had read the Law in the Old Testament, he would have determined again, "Hard it is to be good."

Yet, the wisdom found in the Old Testament and the instructions of the New Testament point to the means or the proper route to the beginning of being good—loving God. The Lord empowers believers to be good through their relationship with Him, thus overcoming the expression, "Hard it is to be good"!

The commandment to love God found in Luke's Gospel.

And behold, a lawyer stood up to put him to the test, saying, "Teacher, what shall I do to inherit eternal life?" He said to him, "What is written in the Law? How do you read it?" And he answered, "You shall love the Lord your God with all your heart and with all your soul and with all your strength and with all your mind, and your neighbor as yourself" (Luke 10:25-27).

What does this imply? Clearly, it describes going deep in one's relationship with God. This happens by having a more intimate relationship with the Spirit. It also points to improving your relationships with others since you are to love your neighbor as yourself.

Loving God improves my relationship with myself. If you cannot get along with yourself, you will find it difficult to get along with others.

First Step: Start with God loving me

Consider what the Scriptures say about God's love for you.

For God so loved the world … (John 3:16).

But God shows his love for us in that while we were still sinners, Christ died for us (Rom 5:8).

In this the love of God was made manifest among us, that God sent his only Son into the world, so that we might live through him. In this is love, not that we have loved God but that he loved us and sent his Son to be the propitiation for our sins. Beloved, if God so loved us, we also ought to love one another (1 John 4:9–11).

Your attitude is a choice. As you accept and apply His love, His instructions transform you. You learn to value people as God values people, which translates into loving one's neighbor as oneself. People who do not value others have an unhealthy self-concept, inviting a lot of drama into their lives.

Think about the order:

1. Love God.
2. Love your neighbor as yourself; i.e., yourself, then your neighbor.

The key to living out the second commandment is living out the first one. If you do not understand loving God, you cannot understand loving yourself. If you do not obey loving God, you cannot love your neighbors as yourself. If you miss number one, you will find it easy to skip number two. If you do not love God, you find it hard to love yourself and so you will have a difficult time loving others. Diotrephes missed this! Where do you miss this?

Your relationship with yourself will be reflected in your relationships with others. The farther you wander from loving God, the farther you wander from loving yourself—and your neighbor. Let me put it this way. Loving others begins with loving God. And loving God begins when we experience His love.

◭ REFLECTION

Where and when do you struggle to be a loving person? The truth is all people struggle.

In what ways do you struggle with self? Selfishness?

In what situations are you critical of yourself?

How do these issues relate to your relationship with God? How do you see God? How do you believe God sees you?

Which lens are you seeing yourself through?

What do you feel about this statement: "Seek to understand before being understood"?

Think about this statement: "Everyone has a different map of the world." How does this statement give you a different perspective of people?

Talk to the Lord about areas that cause you to be self-centered.

Love God. Pursue God. Spend time alone with God.

The second part of the Great Commandment concerning loving one's neighbor as oneself is possible because you have been with God. To focus on loving others, you must focus on how much God loves you. As you love God, you learn to accept who you are—who God made you to be. Then you can truly know yourself as God sees you—His creation, His handiwork.

Accepting who you are helps you to be real—to be yourself—not somebody else. It helps you to quit focusing on what you are not, what you would like to be, or what others expect you to be.

Find out the one thing that makes you unique. When God made you, He made an original. Be the person God made you to be. Then you can be authentic. When you are real, people take notice.

Find who you are in Christ. Accepting who you are in Christ helps you to get past selfishness.

The world teaches people to be more selfish, more self-centered. When you think less about yourself, you discover more about others. It is not thinking less of yourself; it is thinking less about yourself. Then you will discover people think more of you, and better of you.

The ultimate expression of how deeply you love God is reflected in how you interact with other people. You cannot help others or minister to others while you are on the stretcher. Your relationship with God affects your relationships with people. Your relationship with God affects how you look at people. Your attitude toward people affects your witness.

Consider this statement Jesus made, "By this all people will know that you are my disciples, if you have love for one another" (John 13:35). As you love God, you begin to see yourself as God sees you. You allow Him to build character (fruit) in you that aligns with His Word, thus creating a godly influence in your life. The fruit of the Spirit can be seen in the synonyms for unselfish: benevolent, caring, kind, generous, selfless, open-handed, loving, and considerate. You approach significance in your role as a leader as you grow in His love, His grace, His Word, and Christlike character.

Leviticus 19:18 states, "You shall not take vengeance or bear a grudge against the sons of your own people, but you shall love your neighbor as yourself: I am the LORD." If you don't forgive yourself, you most likely will take vengeance on others.

If you are selfish, you have no room for anyone else. A selfish person's conversation is about him- or herself. The most used words in that person's vocabulary is me, my, mine, and I. A selfish person thinks less of others.

Selfless people think of themselves, yet they think of others more. You do not become stuck on yourself and fall victims to the Diotrephes's syndrome in which you like to put yourself first. For Diotrephes, every conversation was about him and what he had done. His motive was to get attention, so he denied those in authority and talked negatively about other leaders. He was one who refused to deny himself and take up his cross. He was the one who did not love his neighbor. Instead, he refused to welcome the brothers. Or maybe he did love his neighbor as himself. It seems he did not get along with himself. He is an example of how the circle of selfishness literally pushes people away.

E. W. Kenyon states in *What Happened from the Cross to the Throne* that the dream of the Father was that love should dominate and rule every one of us.

Selfishness has given birth to all our sorrows, heartaches and tears. It has caused all the wars and other atrocities in which people have taken part. The world is not yet acquainted with the new kind of love—agape love. Few have seen it in practice, and still fewer enjoy its fullness. As believers, our conduct reveals the nature of the Father and His agape love.

Satan's nature is selfishness. God so loved that He gave. Satan was so selfish he sought to rob God and the human race of everything worthwhile. Selfishness is a robber. It reigned without a rival through the ages. Now a mighty new force has broken through. That mighty force is love. It comes from God and is unveiled in Christ. It is becoming operative in us.[8]

This quote had such an impact on my life when I first read it. "Selfishness is a robber." Think about it. It robs you of relationships that encourage you or admonish you. These relationships keep you on track in your spiritual life. Selfishness keeps you from significance. This is why Scripture encourages you to move past selfishness.

Complete my joy by being of the same mind, having the same love, being in full accord and of one mind. Do nothing from selfish ambition or conceit, but in humility count others more significant than yourselves. Let each of you look not only to his own interests, but also to the interests of others (Phil 2:2–4).

"Where does selfishness, or "selfish ambition" show up in your life?"

"Are you looking at the "interests of others?""

Selfishness keeps us self-centered and blurs our vision of others.

The Cure is Simple: Come to Jesus. Deny self. Carry your cross. Follow Him.

One way to see if you are denying yourself is to examine how you listen. As you deny yourself, you become a better listener. That is, you truly listen by paying attention to what others are really saying.

James 1:19 reminds you to "be quick to hear, slow to speak, slow to anger." Listening is developed through curiosity, which explores the deep areas. Proverbs 20:5 says, "The purpose in a man's heart is like deep water, but a man of understanding will draw it out."

Brenda Euland states, "Listening is a magnetic and strange thing, a creative force. The friends who listen to us are the ones we move toward. When we are listened to, it creates us, makes us unfold and expand."[9] Think of a time you added value to someone just by listening.

Stephen Covey comments, "Most people do not listen with the intent to understand; they listen with the intent to reply."[10] Most people in their daily conversations are hearing words, but not listening. They are focused on what they would like to say next, or how they have had a similar experience, or how they were at the same place, or fill-in-the-blank. When phrases like "I have been there" or "I experienced that also" get thrown into the conversation, you begin what one of my mentors calls the fabled "tennis match" and you no longer converse. When you are not focused on the other person through actively listening, you are no longer adding value or encouragement. As Forbes states, "The art of conversation lies in listening."[11]

◬ REFLECTION

Do you make decisions based on how they benefit you or how they benefit others? Explain.

How much would you like someone just to listen to you?

How often do you focus on listening to others?

◬ CHARACTER

Do you work harder at building your image or serving others?

Your love for the Lord is observed in your relationships with others!

Commencement

THE JOURNEY BEGINS AT RESURRECTION

One Friday long ago Jesus cried, "It is finished." The empire of death shouted in triumph.

Silently He passed into the realm of death. That was Friday afternoon.

Then, Sunday morning came. The sun rose and soon many felt it was a different morning.

The disciples soon became aware of the difference. That difference is transformed lives.

> Romans 4:25 (NKJV) states, "He was delivered up for our trespasses He Took our Place and raised for our justification."

He Reconciles us to God. Reconciles means the old account of sin stacked up against you is settled—wiped clean—and you are now reunited with God, who created you. Paul puts it this way in 2 Corinthians 5:17, "Therefore, if anyone is in Christ, he is a new creation; old things have passed away; behold, the new has come."

Watchman Nee reminds believers, "Our old history ends with the cross; our new history begins with the resurrection."[12] The resurrection is the ultimate manifestation of God's saving power, through which believers pass from death to life. Transformed lives is the business Jesus is in.

Resurrection is not just a past event in history, but a present power working in believers' lives today! Thus, one benefit of following Jesus is transformation. This is where the journey to significance begins. Think about what Romans 12:1–2 (NKJV) state.

I beseech you therefore, brethren, by the mercies of God, that you present your bodies a living sacrifice, holy, acceptable to God, which is your reasonable service. And do not be conformed to this world, but be transformed by the renewing of your mind, that you may prove what is that good and acceptable and perfect will of God.

Your values, character, and purpose of life are transformed. You gain a clear understanding of life's purpose. Values change; you value people.

One day I was talking with a man who told me of his work in Alaska. He loved the work, but the men he worked with were pretty rough. He said, "One night I was reading Genesis and the thought hit me that God made these men and is concerned about them. I began looking at these men differently."

When you realize God values people, you begin to value them also. Your perspective changes. You get a fresh perspective. You stop looking for what is wrong in people and take joy in what is right.

⬧ ABUNDANT LIFE

One other benefit of following Jesus that affects your journey to significance is abundant life.

"The thief comes only to steal and kill and destroy."

▲ Your Old Story

"I came that they may have life and have it abundantly."

▲ Your New Story

Which story is yours?

A voice behind you says, "Take the first step." This step will transform your life. You will never be the same if you just begin the journey.

▲ Challenge

Take the first step in the journey to significance. Sharpen your pencil and begin writing your new story.

CHAPTER 2

Milestone: Be Courageous

ROADBLOCK: FEAR

You must be courageous to step into the journey to significance.

A friend of mine, Evangelist Michael Livengood, shared with me a poem his father, H. B. Livengood, used in a sermon on fear:

"The other day upon the stair
I saw a man who wasn't there.
He wasn't there again today.
Oh, how I wish he would go away."[13]

Is your life being controlled by the man on the stair who is not there?

What fear is stopping you from doing the things you should be doing?

How are you handling your fears?

How many people woke up this morning bound to their past—regrets, remorse, even hardness? This kind of past accompanies many people daily.

One woman used to wake up like this every morning. She had a past that kept her bound. Yet because of one man, she was able to rise up with a conscience free from guilt, ready to accomplish what she and other women had planned.

Mary Magdalene and Mary, the mother of James, got up early on Sunday morning to go to the tomb of Jesus to finish the task of embalming His body. Here is one person who did not allow her past to affect the present or prophesy her future. What is really interesting about her story is she is the first person Jesus appears to after His resurrection. She is given a message to tell the rest of His disciples. She is the first person to carry the good news!

Fear will direct you to do things you know you should not do or inspire you to do things you cannot.

One day several years ago, I was caving in the Belt Mountains in Montana with a couple of friends. We had found this cave while hiking one day and decided to come back with the proper equipment. So here we were, entering a cave we knew nothing about. The Spelunking Society of Montana had a sign-in sheet at the entrance of the cave. This should have told us something, yet we entered full force. To enter the cave, we had to shimmy down a log about eight feet long. We turned into an area that looked like a large hallway. We began our exploration.

My friends, Dale and Eric, were looking in another area and were coming to where I was in a few minutes. I spotted a smaller opening on the left side of the hallway. It got my interest and I entered the opening. Suddenly I felt myself sliding down what looked like a large tube. I could not stop. I cannot explain the fear that overcame me at the moment. I was just about scared to death. At the moment I did not know how true that could have been.

I was scratching for anything to hold onto. Finally, I grabbed hold of a small handhold and stopped. My head was spinning. My flashlight had slide in front of me and disappeared. Overwhelming thoughts came to my mind. *Where did the flashlight disappear to? Why couldn't I see a light in front of me? Maybe the flashlight had broken?*

I edged forward, using the extra flashlight I had in my pocket. I found myself sitting right next to the top of an overhang. I found a small stone and dropped it into the darkness. I never heard it hit bottom. A chill ran down my spine. All kinds of thoughts were twirling in my mind. Now I knew what happened to my flashlight and why I did not see a light.

Slowly, I climbed out of the tube and made a mental memo: *Do not go this way!* Interestingly though, I found a military climbing rope at the place I was sitting at the overhang. Lost a flashlight; gained a climbing rope. We found a use for the rope later, but that's another story.

What I learned in this cave has been a life lesson for me: you have to overcome your fear to move out of the hole you are in.

Fear!

Fear of the future.

Fear dominating the present.

Fear of the past.

Therefore the LORD waits to be gracious to you, and therefore he exalts himself to show mercy to you. For the Lord is a God of justice; blessed are all those who wait for him. ... Your ears shall hear a word behind you, saying, 'This is the way, walk in it,' when you turn to the right or when you turn to the left" (Isa 30:18, 21).

Fear keeps you from taking the first step, from taking that step toward the Lord, or to stand for Him! Fear keeps you from opening yourself to others, from being yourself. If you will not allow yourself to be real—to be yourself, people will eventually notice the mask you are wearing.

Whatever you do in life, you will have fear.

Name a time you faced fear and overcame it to do what you needed to do.

When I was in college, I worked on the grounds keeping crew. One of my jobs was to climb trees and cut out the dead limbs and sometimes to reshape the tree. One tree I climbed up about forty feet. I was cutting off a large limb that had been damaged by a storm. I was climbing with a rope and harness and my chain saw was tied with a separate rope. Suddenly, a sheer wind shoved me out of the tree. I dropped my chain saw, which stopped working immediately and fell to the other side of the tree. So far everything was good.

Then the limb I was cutting broke off and came down, hitting me across the face and breaking off a tooth. I climbed down and went back to my dorm. The next day I visited a dentist and started the process of replacing the tooth.

The day after that I went back to work. I was to climb the same tree and finish the job I had started. I had this sudden fear come over me. I did not want to climb that tree. I stood by the trunk of that tree, looking up. Then the thought hit me, "If I don't climb this tree and finish this work, I will never climb again." So, I threw a rope up to a limb and pulled myself up to where I was two days before. I was a little nervous, but I finished the job.

If I had not faced my fears, I would have never climbed again and would have missed out on the wonder and excitement of climbing in the mountains.

What is stopping you from climbing again?

What do you need to do to start again, to face your fears?

Jesus Knows our Fears

Then Jesus said to them, "Do not be afraid. Go and tell My brethren to go to Galilee, and there they will see Me" (Matt 28:10, NKJV).

John 20:11–18 shows Jesus's first concern was that Mary not be afraid. He came to her in the midst of sorrow, confusion, and grief, giving her courage for the next step in the preparation of harvest.

According to F. B. Meyer, "The supreme inquiry for each of us, when summoned to a new work, is not whether we possess sufficient strength or qualification for, but if we have been called of God to do it, and when that is so, there is no further cause for anxiety."[14]

Many People Have Fear Today. Characteristics :

Disabling fear is a sudden overpowering terror that prevents rational thought and action. It often affects many people at once. It causes people to:

Let go. Lie down. Retreat.

Become irrational.

Forget God.

Discourage everyone around them.

The Israelites were backed up against the Red Sea with Pharaoh in hot pursuit. This account is in Exodus 14:10–13 (NKJV):

> And when Pharaoh drew near, the children of Israel lifted their eyes, and behold, the Egyptians marched after them. So they were very afraid, and the children of Israel cried out to the LORD. Then they said to Moses, "Because there were no graves in Egypt, have you taken us away to die in the wilderness? Why have you so dealt with us, to bring us up out of Egypt? Is this not the word that we told you in Egypt, saying, "Let us alone that we may serve the Egyptians?" For it would have been better for us to serve the Egyptians than that we should die in the wilderness."
>
> 13 And Moses said to the people, "Do not be afraid. Stand still, and see the salvation of the LORD, which He will accomplish for you today. For the Egyptians whom you see today, you shall see again no more forever."

Here are the instructions Moses gave to Israel:

1. Get a hold of yourself. Control yourself.
2. Stand still. Take a breath and slow down.
3. Remember God.
4. Be quiet. Don't discourage those around you.

Fear prepares your mind and body for action—sometimes for fight and sometimes for flight. Muscles tense; attention heightens and focuses. Adrenaline is pumped into the system. All this to prepare for some sort of hyperactivity. Yet, for some people, fear produces the very opposite of action. It freezes them into immobility.

Here is a story Jesus taught about investing that illustrates this fear in Matthew 25:24-30 from *The Message*:

> "The servant given one thousand said, ‹Master, I know you have high standards and hate careless ways, that you demand the best and make no allowances for error. I was afraid I might disappoint you, so I found a good hiding place and secured your money. Here it is, safe and sound down to the last cent.'
>
> "The master was furious. ‹That's a terrible way to live! It's criminal to live cautiously like that! If you knew I was after the best, why did you do less than the least? The least you could have done would have been to invest the sum with the bankers, where at least I would have gotten a little interest. " ʻTake the thousand and give it to the one who risked the most. And get rid of this "play-it-safe" who won't go out on a limb. Throw him out into utter darkness.'"

Was his fear a suitable excuse to get him off the hook? Does God consider people unaccountable when fear gains the upper hand and keeps them from doing what they're called to do? No. You must face your fears and overcome.

One church I worked with had gone down to sixty people. Yet they had almost half a million dollars in the bank. One part of the church was adamant that they do not touch the money. "We are saving that for a rainy day!" Another part of the church thought they should be able to use the money for ministry. One person told me she asked a pastor for a CD player to use in children's ministry. She was told, "We have no money to buy a CD player." This fund was a sacred cow that most people were afraid to discuss. Fear was in the room.

I suggested to the board that they look at the money in a healthy way and use it wisely. After some discussion, they decided to budget the money for future use; a portion for an add on to the building, to upkeep their buildings and to use the interest for the different ministries in the church. When the board brought this budget to the church at the annual church business meeting, tension was in the room when the idea was brought up. Though it was on the agenda and they had made the necessary announcements for the business meeting, the board was still hesitant. Because of budget plan for the money and of the way the budget was presented to the members, there was a sigh of relief on both sides of the issue and the budget passed unanimously.

There is more to this story. If I hadn't built trust with the board and with the congregation, this conversation would have never been on the table.

Consider these Scriptures that urge believers to be courageous.

"Have I not commanded you? Be strong and of good courage; do not be afraid, nor be dismayed, for the LORD your God is with you wherever you go" (Josh 1:9, NKJV).

But when Jesus heard it, He answered him, saying, "Do not be afraid; only believe, and she will be made well" (Luke 8:50, NKJV).

"Peace I leave with you, My peace I give to you; not as the world gives do I give to you. Let not your heart be troubled, neither let it be afraid" (John 14:27, NKJV).

▲ MILESTONE: BE COURAGEOUS

Courage Enables You

For God has not given us a spirit of fear, but of power and of love and of a sound mind (2 Tim 1:7, NKJV).

Courage Energizes You

There is no fear in love; but perfect love casts out fear, because fear involves torment. But he who fears has not been made perfect in love (1 John 4:18, NKJV).
To love God deeply energizes you to have courage.

Courage Encourages You

When I am afraid, I put my trust in you. In God, whose word I praise, in God I trust; I shall not be afraid. What can flesh do to me? (Ps 56:3–4).

As the great Danish philosopher Søren Kierkegaard noted: "To dare is to lose one's footing momentarily. To not dare is to lose oneself."[15]

Be on guard. Stand firm in the faith; Be courageous. Be strong (1 Cor 16:13, NLT).."

Remember these words of Jesus:

In the Book of Revelation, John reminds believers of the words of Jesus. When you face your fear, remember these powerful words:

And when I saw Him, I fell at His feet as dead. But He laid His right hand on me, saying to me, "Do not be afraid; I am the First and the Last. I am He who lives, and was dead, and behold, I am alive forevermore. Amen. And I have the keys of Hades and of Death" (Rev 1:17–18, NJKV).

◣ 1. "Do Not Be Afraid."

C. S. Lewis writes, "Courage is not simply one of the virtues, but the form of every virtue on its testing point."[16]

◣ 2. "I Am the First and the Last"

He is still "the first and the last."

He is the eternal, unchanging Christ.

Jesus Christ is the same yesterday, today, and forever (Heb 13:8, NKJV).

Time changes you, but Jesus is beyond time. And He is above your circumstances.

You must be determined. In Him you find stability.

You must always be challenged to move on a little further. In Him you have the strength to continue the journey.

He is preparing you for eternity.

◣ 3. "I Am He Who Lives, and Was Dead, and Behold, I am Alive Forevermore, Amen."

He is the Living One (a title for God)!

And Joshua said, "By this you shall know that the living God is among you ..." (Josh 3:10, NKJV).

As the deer pants for the water brooks, So pants my soul for You, O God. My soul thirsts for God, for the living God (Ps 42:1–2a, NKJV).

As the Living One, God is your source of life and healing. Do you know Him?

For I, the LORD your God, will hold your right hand, Saying to you, "Fear not, I will help you" (Isa 41:13, NKJV).

4. I have the Keys to Hades and of Death» .”

Keys are a symbol of authority.

And Jesus came and spoke to them, saying, "All authority has been given to Me in heaven and on earth" (Matt 28:18, NKJV).

Jesus Christ is in control!

"Alleluia! For the Lord God Omnipotent reigns!" (Revelation 19:6, NKJV).

He holds the keys to the kingdom of God!

When you are about to turn around because the flow is too great, keep going forward. His strength will sustain you.

Remember. Because God reigns, you do not have to fear.

When you need healing and you don't know where to turn, turn to Jesus, the Great Physician.

Remember. God reigns!

When you are so low you can see bottom, be encouraged.

Remember. God reigns!

When you are about to give up, don't.

Remember. God reigns!

He still reigns when people feel there is no God.

He still reigns when you are in the middle of a trial.

He still reigns when death seems to be swallowing you up.

Yea, though I walk through the valley of the shadow of death, I will fear no evil, for You are with me … (Ps 23:4, NKJV).

He still reigns when governments are crumbling.

He still reigns when the economy falls.

He still reigns when vision is gone.

He still reigns when people defy His holy Name.

Daniel prayed three times daily when it was illegal to pray. Daniel was thrown into the lion's den. But the Lord was with Him. Remember. God reigns!

He still reigns when you see the enemy encamped about you, when you feel the enemy has surrounded you. The Lord reigns!

Remember Elisha when the army of Syria had surrounded him? The army of the Lord was between him and his enemies (2 Kgs 6).

E. Stanley Jones says, "I am inwardly fashioned for faith, not for fear. Fear is not my native land; faith is. I am so made that worry and anxiety are sand in the machinery of life; faith is the oil."[17]

You will live better by faith and confidence than by fear, doubt, and anxiety.

Fear not, for I have redeemed you; I have called you by name, you are mine. When you pass through the waters, I will be with you; and through the rivers, they shall not overwhelm you (Isa 43:1b–2a).

Every time you refuse to take the difficult step, each time you keep quiet instead of saying the hard word, you die a little. And your faith dies a little too as your fear whispers to you that God is not really big enough to take care of you.

Something Important Happens Every Time We Face Our Fears.

Each time you face a fearful challenge and act, you will get a little stronger inside. You become more alive. You trust God more.

Take the step into the realm of fear. You will be amazed at the journey you are beginning.   Because of fear, people do not trust God.

Because of fear, they find it difficult to come to God in their time of need.

Jesus says, "Do not be afraid."

Come to Jesus. He will give you courage to overcome the fear that blocks leadership decisions and actions. With God's assurance, you can move forward to lead in ways that positively affects the work in your church or business.

You can make a difference in the lives of others by taking courage and overcoming your fear.

CHAPTER 3

Milestone: Be Calm

ROADBLOCK: STRESS

Then, the same day at evening, being the first day of the week, when the doors were shut where the disciples were assembled, for fear of the Jews, Jesus came and stood in the midst, and said to them, "Peace be with you" (John 20:19, NKJV).

Calm and peace are opposites of inner turmoil and stress. Calmness is:

> freedom from inner storms
> freedom from agitation
> freedom to be yourself
> freedom to enjoy the moment
> untroubled
> even tempered
> in control of self.

Calm is the peace comes as a result of reconciliation and forgiveness!

I was hiking with my family at a State Park. We had just sat down at a picnic table and were about to eat lunch when my phone rang. I looked at the number and knew it was a pastor calling me. I walked away from my family and answered the phone. The voice at the other end sounded shaken. He had gotten a letter from someone in the congregation and it shook him up a little.

He read the letter to me. I smiled as I encouraged him that the letter was not how most people felt. I encouraged him to talk to the person with another trusted individual in the room with him. I also said to him when Paul had opposition, Paul felt it told him he was doing what God wanted him to do. When working for the Lord, one will come across opposition! I shared with him about men who did not like me when I first arrived at a church, and even told me so. But after some time these men became my greatest supporters. After talking a few minutes, I prayed with him. The Pastor said he felt better.

When I walked back to my family, my son asked me what was that all about. I told him it was another reason I'm glad I'm not pastoring anymore.

How Do You Deal With Difficult People.

Here are a few thoughts.

Deal with yourself first. Find God's peace and apply it in your life. The most difficult person I have had to deal with in my life was not the person who stuck an unsigned letter under my door; it was me.

Romans 5:1 states, "Therefore, since we have been justified by faith, we have peace with God through our Lord Jesus Christ." As you discover, or rediscover, God's forgiveness, that peace with God, gives you peace within, which helps you to come to grips with forgiving yourself.

Peace and harmony can be achieved by forgiving, encouraging, and staying connected with people.

▲ FORGIVE YOURSELF FIRST

John Maxwell has written:

"The first person I must know is myself; This brings self-awareness.

The first person I must get along with is myself;

This leads to a healthy image.

The first person to cause me problems is myself;

Admitting truth yields self-honesty.

The first person I must change is myself;

This empowering attitude paths the way to self improvement."[18]

The first person you must forgive is yourself. This leads to peace within and forgiveness of others.

As you wander in life, let this be your goal. Keep your eye on the donut, not on the hole.

So many things keep you from keeping the priority you need. Here is the donut:

You keep him in perfect peace whose mind is stayed on you, because he trusts in you (Isa 26:3).

Fixing Your Mind On Christ Fixes Your Mind

Here is where you begin to lay the foundation:

Do not be conformed to this world, but be transformed by the renewal of your mind, that by testing you may discern what is the will of God, what is good and acceptable and perfect (Rom 12:2).

Keeping your mind on Jesus transforms—renews—your mind. As you trust God, you begin to see yourself differently.

Consider the lyrics from a song by the Imperials, "From the start you built a place in my heart, a place that no one else could fill. But sin kept Your Spirit from working in me. I couldn't look at life honestly."[19] You cannot look at life honestly or live in a realm of peace if you constantly struggle with forgiveness!

John Maxwell shared in a training session, "People won't go along with you if they can't get along with you." And you will not get along with others if you cannot get along with yourself.

A lot of people do not have that loving, trusting relationship with themselves. Many are much more critical of themselves than they are of others. They will give other people the benefit of the doubt, but won't give themselves any slack at all.

Consider what the Scriptures teach about forgiveness.

Be kind to one another, tenderhearted, forgiving one another, as God in Christ forgave you (Eph 4:32).

He has delivered us from the domain of darkness and transferred us to the kingdom of his beloved Son, in whom we have redemption, the forgiveness of sins (Col 1:13–14).

Love your neighbor. Be kind to your neighbor. Forgive your neighbor.

Love yourself. Be kind to yourself. Forgive yourself.

If you cannot get along with yourself, you cannot, will not, get along with others. If you struggle with forgiving yourself, you will struggle forgiving others. This is particularly true in regard to the sin you struggle with.

Forgiving yourself after God has forgiven you is foundational to trusting God. For many people, this is the hardest hurdle to cross in gaining trust in others. If you do not trust yourself, can you trust another? If you do not trust yourself, people will spot it while you walk across the street from them. People will see it in your demeanor.

The key to trusting yourself is loving God and trusting in Him. You will have difficulty loving and trusting God if you are dragging your past around all the time. Listen to what Romans 8:1 teaches:

There is therefore now no condemnation for those who are in Christ Jesus. Quit hanging on to past, the old way of life. Hang on to God. Quit putting yourself down. Start seeing yourself as free in Christ. Quit listening to those thoughts that put you down day after day, such as, "I'm not good enough." Instead, listen to God's Word. Quit living in your past. Walk in the Spirit. Yesterday ended last night! Quit Dragging the past around with you.

For those who live according to the flesh set their minds on the things of the flesh, but those who live according to the Spirit set their minds on the things of the Spirit. For to set the mind on the flesh is death, but to set the mind on the Spirit is life and peace (Rom 8:5–6).

I am convinced that as people struggle with unforgiveness, the more selfish they become. When your thoughts are always on your struggle, it keeps you locked up in the prison of self. Corrie Ten Boom speaks to this through these thought provoking words, "Forgiveness is the key that unlocks the door of resentment and the handcuffs of hatred. It is a power that breaks the Chains of Bitterness and the shackles of selfishness." [20]

The more you struggle, the more selfish you become. You cannot erase the past. You must let it go. You cannot walk away from yourself, but you can let it go. How?

First, God's law of forgiveness instructs you how to let it go. Leviticus 16 provides instruction about the Day of Atonement. Two goats are selected from the congregation and lots are cast. The one whose lot is cast for the Lord is offered for a sin offering. Aaron laid hands on the live goat, confessing the sins of the camp. The goat is sent into the wilderness as a scapegoat. Listen to how Moses describes this.

The goat shall bear all their iniquities on itself to a remote area, and he shall let the goat go free in the wilderness (Lev 16:22).

Second, Paul's advice is to let it go. Do not walk according to the flesh. Stop it. Interestingly, Paul adds another instruction: Walk in the Spirit. Keep your thoughts on Jesus. Spend time with God every day.

For many, however, living in the past becomes comfortable. It is safe territory. It is safe because people have this tendency to distort the story to keep it safe. They try to justify their part, allowing the negative elements to be pushed deeper into their subconscious.

I followed a pastor whose philosophy about problems was that if he ignores them, they would go away. Well, he did ignore them, but they did not go away. The fact is they became greater problems.

You can overlook your past, but, in reality, you are pushing it deeper into your subconscious where it is hidden until a certain sound, picture, smell or taste brings it forward, causing an avalanche of emotions to tear into you. Instead, you need to deal with it. Repent. Then don't go back there.

Lewis Smedes put it this way, "If forgiving ourselves comes easy, chances are we are only excusing ourselves, ducking blame, and not really forgiving ourselves at all."[21]

Forgiving yourself is a voluntary, emotional, and intentional process that brings a change of feelings and attitude regarding an offense.

▲ START FOCUSING ON JESUS

Focus is a cognitive process in which you selectively concentrating on one aspect of the environment while ignoring other things.

> "Turn your eyes upon Jesus
> Look full in His wonderful face
> and the things of earth
> will grow strangely dim
> In the light of His Glory and Grace."
> - Lyrics by Helen Howarth Lemmel[22]

Turning Your Eyes Upon Jesus Fixes Your Mind.

You cannot turn your eyes on Jesus and keep looking at your offense.

When you know the past record of others, their sin of the past, and you define that person today for what they did years ago, you are passing judgment.

The real hurdle to cross is you know your own past and you tend to define yourself by your past. Yes, you are judging yourself, but because you do not receive God's forgiveness and forgive yourself, you build limiting beliefs that are hindering you from following Jesus.

Your limiting beliefs about yourself keep you from moving higher; keep you from victory. They keep you from having close relationships.

Let It Go And Fix Your Mind On Jesus

Have you ever told yourself, "I can't do that?"

Have you ever thought, *I'm not good, so I can never … .*

These may be limiting beliefs brought on by you not forgiving yourself or brought on by someone's words.

Counting and recounting the hurts of your past keep you stuck in a rut of self-bitterness.

Change your limiting belief about yourself with God's help.

There comes a time when you have to intentionally decide to stop beating yourself up over the mistakes you made in the past.

Do you use a calendar app on your cell phone, tablet or computer? Get it out and make this appointment with yourself, "Stop beating myself up."

⚠ Onion Principle

Every time you peel an onion, there is an emotional response—tears in your eyes. Each layer removed brings its own response, though diminishing the size and diluting its effect on your senses. It is a process.

Forgiving oneself is a process, not an event. It is peeling the onion. Every time you forgive yourself, the inner critic, your gremlin's voice becomes weaker and weaker, diluting its effect on you.

You must come to the realization God has forgiven you and becasue He has forgiven you, you may forgive yourself. Forgiving yourself is an intentional process. Don't give up! You will make it to the other side: real freedom is waiting there.

David's Confession:
For I acknowledge my transgressions, and my sin is always before me (Ps 51:3, NKJV).

David's Prayer:
Create in me a clean heart, O God, and renew a steadfast spirit within me. Do not cast me away from Your presence, And do not take Your Holy Spirit from me. Restore to me the joy of Your salvation, and uphold me by Your generous Spirit (Ps 51:10–12, NKJV).

An Imperials' song powerfully speaks of forgiveness. "I know this love You placed in my heart is a love that will never depart. Sin brought me here to the end of my rope. But now you've given me a brand new hope. I'm forgiven."[23]

You may be struggling with a voice within, an inner critic, and you realize you need to quiet this voice. Admit it and come face-to-face with your gremlin. Don't allow it to speak so loud. It is your inner critic. Confront it.

Keep doing this and you will find, as if pealing an onion layer by layer, the voice within becomes quieter. It is not as abrasive as before. You become the master instead of the gremlin by fixing your mind on Jesus.

When the accuser says you failed, admit it and tell him you are learning from it.

When the accuser says you can't do this, tell him with time you will get better.

When the accuser says you're not good enough, tell him, "God says I am good enough, and He is improving me daily."

When the accuser brings up an old sin, tell him you're forgiven. God has set you free.

When you forgive yourself, you open the door and walk out of prison in freedom.

▲ FIXING YOUR MIND ON JESUS, FIXES YOUR MIND

The Lord is at hand; do not be anxious about anything, but in everything by prayer and supplication with thanksgiving let your requests be made known to God. And the peace of God, which surpasses all understanding, will guard your hearts and your minds in Christ Jesus. Finally, brothers, whatever is true, whatever is honorable, whatever is just, whatever is pure, whatever is lovely, whatever is commendable, if there is any excellence, if there is anything worthy of praise, think about these things.

What you have learned and received and heard and seen in me—practice these things, and the God of peace will be with you (Phil 4:5b–9). A lack of forgiveness produces stress.

Jesus instructed in Matthew 5:23–24, "If you bring your gift to the altar, and there remember that your brother has something against you, leave your gift there before the altar, and go your way. First be reconciled to your brother, and then come and offer your gift" (NKJV).

Once, when giving communion, I noticed a board member passing on the emblems, not taking them for himself. I was in conversation with him sometime later and asked him how he was doing. I shared with him that I noticed he did not partake of communion earlier in the month. He looked at me surprised. I quietly said, "If you don't want to talk about it, we can talk about something else." He explained that as he was reaching to receive the emblems, he had something in his heart against someone and just passed the emblems to his wife and did not partake himself. He went to the person and made things right.

There are times when you come close to God that He will nudge you, reminding you there is someone you need to forgive or ask for forgiveness.

Have you had this experience when you were about to take communion? How did you handle it? What did you do?

If you do not respond to the Lord's nudge to go to someone, you become miserable.

As long as your mind is stayed on yourself, your own selfish ways, you will never have peace. You may have seen a plaque or poster with these words: "When momma's not happy, nobody's happy." When momma's not happy, there will be stress.

When you are miserable, you make sure no one else is happy. You want people to be like you and join in on your misery.

When you are around a person like this, he or she plays on fear, trying to make sure you are living in the realm of stress also. "Misery loves company."

However, your happiness is not other peoples responsibility. It is your responsibility. It is an attitude. It is a choice.

Do you keep this type of company?

Are you like this?

"There is no peace," says the LORD, "for the wicked" (Is 48:22).

There is no calm in the life of those who dive into wickedness. Stress reigns in their minds.

▲ REFLECTION

Are you upset with someone?

Have you asked for forgiveness recently for something you have done to upset others?

▲ DEALING WITH UNEXPECTED OR DIFFICULT SITUATIONS

God does not promise an easy life without challenges or pain. Stress can come when you worry about how to deal with a new, scary, difficult, or painful situation. Paul had many difficult encounters and situations as he preached the gospel to the Philippians. Yet he instructed them (and all believers) to be thankful and to rejoice in all types of difficulties.

Rejoice in the Lord always. Again I will say, rejoice! Let your gentleness be known to all men. The Lord is at hand. Be anxious for nothing, but in everything by prayer and supplication, with thanksgiving, let your requests be made known to God; and the peace of God, which surpasses all understanding, will guard your hearts and minds through Christ Jesus (Phil 4:4–7, NKJV).

James writes this advice to believers:

Count it all joy, my brothers, when you meet trials of various kinds, for you know that the testing of your faith produces steadfastness. And let steadfastness have its full effect, that you may be perfect and complete, lacking in nothing (Jas 1:2–4).

The English word for peace means absence of trouble. Freedom from war, hostility, disturbance, quarrels, mental/spiritual conflict. But peace is not a mere absence of strife. If you clear a plot of land of all weeds, you do not have a garden, you have a barren field.

I read once that the Hebrew word shalom means completeness, to be complete, safe, sound, order, and well-being. So when someone says shalom to you, that person is really saying is. "In your life, may you have order and well-being."

May you have a sense of security. May you have a sense of a foundation underneath your feet.

Stress, or the lack of peace, will most likely become a roadblock in your journey to having a significant impact on your success when working.

STORY OF STORM IN GIBSON CITY

A church I pastored needed a new roof. The building was old and had the original roof. Twenty-five people were attending the church, but we could not afford to pay for a new roof, even though the roof was leaking.

I prayed and asked God to help us replace the roof. Nancy and I drove to a meeting in Urbana, Illinois, about thirty miles away. As we were driving home, we saw a tornado approaching our community. Storms come and go, and we had come to realize we could not control the storms. Nancy and I were in a car that was shaking, but a calm swept over us. When we arrived to our home that was next to the church building, we noticed part of the church's roof was missing. I called our insurance company the next day! God had answered prayer in an unusual way.

Another church I pastored averaged one humdred forty before we came. A few years later, the church was averaging almost three hundred. Then my sister Jerri Beth found out she had cancer. My father had a stroke and we had to put him in a nursing home. One day I left my office to visit a man whose wife came to our church. He was depressed. I remember sitting in the car, looking at his front door. I could not get out of the car. I had tears flowing down my face. I had not realized how depressed I was myself. I had tears running down my face as I drove home instead of going back to the office.

A few months earlier, I had been offered a sabbatical, but did not take it because I felt I had too much to do. Now I found myself stressed out, depressed, and burned out! I made an appointment with a doctor who put me on depression medication that I took for about 9 months. I began seeing a counselor, who was a member of our church.

Looking back, I brought much of this stress on myself. I was not getting the proper rest. I was working long hours in the ministry of the church. But I was seeking God less and less.

Since that time, I have made a greater regiment in my devotional life and spending time with God. I probably still need improvement. I am a high D in the DISC assessment, and a D's motto is get it done.

Stress due to overwork can be a roadblock. You need to find your peace in God instead of in your work.

▲ Four Instructions to Develop Peace in Your Life

1. "You will keep in him perfect peace, whose mind is stayed on you: because he trusts in you (Isa 26:3, NKJV).

The only way to peace of mind is to trust the Lord for your situation.

Notice these incredible words from Isaiah 48:17–18:

"This is what the Lord says—your Redeemer, the Holy One of Israel: I am the Lord your God, who teaches you what is best for you, who directs you in the way you should go. If only you had paid attention to my commands, your peace would have been like a river, your well-being like the waves of the sea" (NIV).

Keep your mind on the Lord. You sometimes forget you can fill your mind with whatever you choose. Practice peace by your keeping your mind on the Lord.

I have noticed when someone says something negative to me or criticizes me for some reason, it often brings to memory something negative from the past and puts me on guard. Peace seems to fade away with stress taking its place.

I have found it better to ask the person if we can talk about the issue at some other time to allow myself time to become calm before responding. How you answer someone is a choice. When you answer is also a choice!

What you think and do is a matter of the will. You can choose either stress or peace! You choose to be part of the drama or to be in another play, with a role of being calm.

A Matter of Choice

"Choose this day whom you will serve" (Josh 24:15). When you begin your day, you choose your attitude for the rest of the day. Your choice depends on who or what you are thinking about.

What did you think about when you woke up this morning?

Who influenced your thoughts?

How did it affect your attitude?

Be aware that your thoughts affect your attitude and your attitude has an effect on your day. Choose Jesus. He brings peace. Don't just think about it; make it a matter of the heart.

2. "Let the peace of Christ rule in your hearts" (Col 3:15).

How do you let the peace of God rule in your heart?

Paul tells the believers in Colosse to (1) forbear one another, and (2) forgive one another.

If one has a complaint against another, forgiving each other; as the Lord has forgiven you, so you also must forgive. And above all these put on love, which binds everything together in perfect harmony (Col 3:13–14).

Mrs. Will Murphy writes these words in the hymn "Constantly Abiding": There's a peace in my heart that the world never gave, a peace it cannot take away;

> Tho' the trials of life may surround like a cloud,
> I've a peace that has come there to stay.
> All the world seemed to sing of a Savior and King,
> When peace sweetly came to my heart;
> Troubles all fled away
> and my night turned to day,
> Blessed Jesus, how glorious Thou art! [24]

3. "Seek peace and pursue it" (Ps 34:14).

Therefore, let us pursue the things which make for peace and the things by which one may edify another (Rom 14:19, NKJV).

Pursue peace with all people, and holiness, without which no one will see the Lord (Heb 12:14, NKJV).

An unknown author has penned the poem, *Be Still.*

> Lord, keep me still,
> Though stormy waves may blow
> And waves my little vessel may overflow,
> Or even in the darkness I must go;
> Lord, keep me still.
>
> The waves are in Thy hand,
> The roughest seas subside at Thy command.
> Steer Thou my vessel in safety to the land
> And keep me still,
> Keep me still.[25]

Peace is a calmness of mind that is not ruffled by adversity, overclouded by a remorseful conscience, or disturbed by fear.

4. Be a peacemaker.

Now the fruit of righteousness is sown in peace by those who make peace (Jas 3:18, NKJV).

You don't find peace with others; you make it. It comes from one who has peace within.

You must realize that being a peacemaker means you must go through troubled water to bring about peace. A peacemaker refuses to be part of the problem. A peacemaker does not think of him- or herself first, but is concerned for others.

Yet you must not settle for peace at any cost, such as compromising your faith.

"Peace won by compromise is usually short-lived achievement," according to Winfield Scott. [26]

Sir Thomas Fuller declared, "It is madness for sheep to talk peace with a wolf."[27]

Yet there is a cost for peace. I have learned and experienced if you want to go higher in the Lord or in relationships, you must give up certain rights and take up responsibility. A person who only thinks of his or her rights will never be a peacemaker, and probably does not have a calm spirit. Keeping your rights is living in a realm of stress.

Here is the key word: responsibility. Take responsibility for your life. You begin to look at people differently in the realm of taking responsibility for your actions—much differently than in the realm of demanding your rights.

Taking responsibility is accompanied by calm. Demanding rights is accompanied by stress.

In which realm are you living?

To grow up, you must give up. To be the man or woman God wants you to be, you must willing give up rights and take up responsibility for your actions.

▲ REFLECTION

Do you have peace?

Are you living in the realm of calm?

Wonderful Peace is a hymn written by W. G. Cooper.
Far away in the depths of my spirit tonight
rolls a melody sweeter than psalm.
In celestial like strains
it unceasingly falls
O'er my soul like an infinite calm.
Peace! Peace! Wonderful peace,
Coming down from the Father above.
Sweep over my spirit forever I pray,
in fathomless billows of love.

> What a treasure
> I have in this wonderful peace,
> Buried deep in the heart of my soul.
> So secure that no power
> can mine it away,
> While the years of eternity roll.[28]

Paul writes to the Corinthians, "Finally, brethren, farewell. Become complete. Be of good comfort, be of one mind, live in peace; and the God of love and peace will be with you" (2 Cor 13:11, NKJV).

You can make a difference in the lives of others by living in God›s peace.

CHAPTER 4

Milestone: Be Confident

ROADBLOCKS: INSECURITY, DOUBT

Many people today lack belief in people. It may come from a lack of belief in themselves! The root problem comes from the lack of belief in God, how people view God and think about God.

Do you believe in God?

Are you aware that God loves you? God believes in you! He values you! He has offered you grace.

Where does your belief in God contradict with your belief in your ability in what God is calling you to do?

Do you believe in the people around you? How do you view yourself? How does God view you?

How does your belief in God affect how you live?

A friend, Scott Green, described how his belief in God affected his life in this way. "It affects my seeing things on an eternal scale (perception). Knowing God has things under control."

What effect does your belief have on you? Does it give confidence, lower stress, build faith and endurance? What else?

First of all, remember John 3:16. "For God so loved the world ... ." When you come to grips with God's love for you and His desire to have a relationship with you, then you realize God has a purpose for your life.

God's Word will help change your unbelief in God, yourself,

and others to help you achieve the milestone of confidence. You need to truly believe and have confidence in God's will and authority in the world and in your life. The stronger your confidence is in God's authority, the more confident you can be in the work He asks you to do with people in your church or business.

"And Jesus came and spoke to them, saying, 'All authority has been given to Me in heaven and on earth'" (Matt 28:18, NKJV).

Authority has been defined as "The power or right to perform certain acts without impediment."[29]

Where have you worked for someone who gave you freedom to do the work you were assigned using your own strengths and giftings? How did that make you feel?

When have you worked for someone who was a micromanager who needed to approval almost everything you did before you could move on? How did you feel working here?

I read once that people don't leave companies, they leave managers. I believe this is an accurate perspective.

Pastors and leaders need to give people under them room to grow and to be themselves, instead of someone leaders would like to make them. I appreciate the people I have worked for in the past who allowed me to be me.

Who can you thank for being a good boss?

Lawrence Richards defines authority like this: "The basic idea in the word, 'authority' is freedom of choice. The greater the authority, the greater the possibility of unrestricted freedom of action. And the person without authority has little freedom of action, for others maintain a right to control him and determine what he does."[30]

God the Father gave Christ authority (Matt 28:18). The Greek for authority (*exousia*) refers to delegated authority. Jesus had authority when He was on earth. People were amazed and glorified God when they observed the authority Jesus had.

Everything Jesus did and said He did with the authority God

gave Him. "Do you not believe that I am in the Father and the Father in me? The words that I speak to you I do not speak on My own authority; but the Father who dwells in Me does the works" (John 14:10–11, NKJV). Jesus worked under the authority of His Father while He was ministering to people on earth before His crucifixion.

Jesus also sent His disciples out at certain times in their training to do the work of ministry. Interestingly, when He sent them out, He gave them these instructions according to Luke 9:1-2. "And he called the twelve together and gave them power and authority over all demons and to cure diseases, and he sent them out to proclaim the kingdom of God and to heal."

When He calls believers to do His work, He sends them out also. The Great Commission is to go and make disciples. Go is a sending direction.

God gives each believer different gifts to do His work. When you do the work of the ministry in the gifts the Lord gives, you do the work in the authority of the One who gave the gift.

And He gives the Holy Spirit to guide believers, according to John 16:13. "However, when He, the Spirit of truth, has come, He will guide you into all truth; for He will not speak on His own authority, but whatever He hears He will speak; and He will tell you things to come." (NKJV).

⚠ REFLECTION

How did you feel the last time the Holy Spirit nudged you or you heard the Holy Spirit tell you to witness to someone?

How did you respond?

Did your heart race?

Did you feel a loss of words?

I remember witnessing on the streets of Tampa, Florida, one Saturday afternoon, I began listening to a girl as she witnessed to a huge gang member. She looked up at him and said, "God see's you when you cry yourself to sleep at night."

He looked around, then asked, "Who told you?"

She said, "Jesus." He listened to her share a simple gospel message and prayed through to salvation. I heard he later became a pastor.

Words come to you in the moment.

———————————————

All this is tied directly to confidence!

God is living within you. The Holy Spirit is within you and with you, but you still find it difficult to live for Jesus, to trust that the Holy Spirit will help you live for God, and to guide or help others to live for God.

Many Christians fail to live for Jesus because they do not realize their true identity in Christ. And they do not step out in the work God has called them to do.

When I moved to Carlinville and became the new pastor, I was told by many pastors in the district that they could not pastor there because of all the district leaders and ministers in the church. (There were twenty-nine ordained ministers in the church.)

I was sitting on the platform the first Sunday Nancy and I were called to this ministry. I was looking at men who had mentored me and I whispered to God, "What in the world am I doing here? There are several men here who could pastor this church better than me!" A voice within me rose up and said, *You can't do this.* But God clearly spoke to me, "I did not call those men to pastor this church. I called you." From the moment I heard His voice, I had confidence to do what He called me to do. He had called me specifically. He had delegated authority to me to carry on His work of encouraging and building up the people in that church. God gave my wife and me fruitful ministry because we worked in delegated authority.

When God empowers you to do His work, confidence is the by-product. When God empowers, He develops your ability to carry out His work.

You may not know how until you step out in the confidence zone.

This means leaving your comfort zone to walk by faith. Step out of your comfort zone and do what God calls you to do, even if you are not fully trained.

After the initial training, and perhaps Bible college and seminary, the real training begins as you lean on God! God becomes your guide and mentor, and He puts people in your life to assist you.

My first assignment in ministry was in Mascoutah, Illinois. Pastor Larry Griswold asked me to be his assistant pastor. He assigned certain job responsibilities. I added one: minister to a college in Belleville, Illinois, with Dan Bell, a youth pastor in the area.

My training for ministry continued as I worked with Pastor Griswold. He mentored me and I learned much from my time with him. He also encouraged me to grow more by taking me to trainings available in the area. Notice I wrote taking me. He did not send me; he took me with him. Some people are event coordinators, sending you to trainings in the area. Others are guides taking you to trainings.

▲ REFLECTION

As a pastor or business owner or leader, how are you developing your staff?

Who are you mentoring right now?

Who is mentoring you?

Is training for staff in your budget? If not, how can you begin setting aside funds for training?

There are principles to follow as you step out and do what God is asking you to do. He comes alongside (another milestone: companion) and helps you do what He asks.

When you are following His commands, you are under His authority, which gives you the confidence you need to fulfill what He is asking you to do. His authority is the umbrella of protection and freedom you work under. As a result of working in this environment of trust and security, you develop further confidence to accomplishing the task.

▲ REFLECTION

Do you have that kind of confidence?

Where does insecurity appear in your life?

Where do you lack confidence?

Who can you find to help you overcome this roadblock?

When are you going to contact them?

Some things you cannot do by yourself. But notice that He gives you a task to carry out and the freedom to carry it out.

What causes you to settle for less?

When you come under His authority, it is seen in your obedience.

Dr. Dan Reiland serves as the executive pastor at 12 Stone Church in Lawrenceville, Georgia. I look forward to receiving his email I subscribe to, danreiland.com. He wrote this about the transference of authority: "Authority is always transferred. Even Jesus' authority was transferred to Him from the Father."

Take a look at Matthew 28:18–20. "And Jesus came and said to them, 'All authority in heaven and on earth has been given to me. Go therefore and make disciples of all nations ….'"

Now read John 10:17–18. "For this reason the Father loves me, because I lay down my life that I may take it up again. No one takes it from me, but I lay it down of my own accord. I have authority to lay it down, and I have authority to take it up again. This charge I have received from my Father."

It is not difficult to see Jesus acknowledging His source of authority.

What happens then?

Jesus transfers His authority to the disciples. You have already seen this in Matthew 28.

Consider also Luke 9:1–2. "And he called the twelve together and gave them power and authority over all demons and to cure diseases, and he sent them out to proclaim the kingdom of God and to heal."

Dr. Reiland makes this analogy:

> If my 14-year-old son John-Peter told his 16-year-old sister to clean her room, she would more likely "clean his clock." If, however, John-Peter had said, "Mackenzie, Mom says you have to clean your room," the room will soon be clean. What is the difference? Authority was transferred from mom to John-Peter!
>
> Whenever you forget the source of your authority and begin to believe it is yours, you move from "I am responsible" to "I have my rights," and trouble begins.
>
> Responsibility is Key!
> When self-confidence is greater than God's confidence, watch out! When you have confidence in God, He helps you have a balanced self-confidence.
>
> Sustaining Authority
> Your ability to sustain transferred authority is entirely dependent upon your faithfulness to serve the one who gives you the authority.[31]

◢ THE HOLY SPIRIT MAKES US ABLE TO MINISTER

The Holy Spirit employs you in the authority of Jesus to accomplish the work. Working under His authority gives you the confidence to continue.

Paul reminds believers that God "has made us sufficient to be ministers of a new covenant, not of the letter but of the Spirit. For the letter kills, but the Spirit gives life" (2 Cor 3:6). You must trust God's ability to make you able to do what He has called you to do.

If you knew you would be successful, what would you start doing right now?

◢ FACING OUR DOUBTS

"The simple believes everything, but the prudent gives thought to his steps" (Prov 14:15).

There are always those who instill doubt into our minds.

One of the disciples of Jesus was known for his struggle with doubt. You are already ahead of me. That's right, it was Doubting Thomas. Doubt almost destroyed him. Yet he rose above his doubts to serve Jesus to the end of his life. Thomas's story is found in John 20:19–25. What made Thomas doubt? He was not in the room with the other disciples when Jesus came the first time. That doubt quickly vanished when Thomas personally witnessed the resurrected Jesus.

Are you struggling with doubts? In my life I have struggled through doubts. I struggled with what my parents and my church believed, taught, and lived. My doubts drove me into God's Word, which turned my doubts to strong belief. I moved from doubting to believing, from believing to living it out, from living it to sharing it with others.

Strong beliefs develop values. Borrowed beliefs have little influence—no real power—in your life until they become your beliefs.

All people have doubts. They have doubts about relationships. They doubt if anyone cares for them. They have doubts about God.

God is not driven away by your doubts. Doubt is struggling with unbelief. Unbelief is a choice. Doubt literally means to withdraw, hesitate, or waver.

The doubt the disciples and Thomas struggled with was the Resurrection. Jesus had told them He would be crucified, that He would die. He also explained to them that on the third day He would rise again. They heard the first part about death and did not like it. They probably did not hear or misunderstood the second part about resurrection. What they needed was hope. Without His resurrection hope, Christianity does not make sense. Power exists in the Resurrection for everyday living.

◢ REFLECTION

Do you fully grasp the reality of Jesus's resurrection in your life?

Where do you work on making this realization a part of your life?

What Scriptures can you read or memorize to help you?

When are you going to set aside more time to spend with God?

Date: Time: _____

Jesus was arrested, then crucified In this one dark moment, the disciples lost their way. Commitment is hard to keep when your dreams are crucified before your very eyes.

Let's go back about two and a half years. When the Twelve were sent out, Thomas was with them, healing the sick, casting out evil spirits, and preaching the good news.

The Scriptures record Thomas speaking three times. The first time Thomas speaks is when Jesus and the disciples are journeying to see Lazarus after his death. At this point, the pharisees are looking for a way to kill Jesus.

"Then after this he said to the disciples, 'Let us go to Judea again.' The disciples said to him, 'Rabbi, the Jews were just now seeking to stone you, and are you going there again?' So Thomas, called the Twin, said to his fellow disciples, 'Let us also go, that we may die with Him' " (John 11:7, 8, 16).

Can you hear Thomas singing, "I have decided to follow Jesus. No turning back"?

The second time Thomas speaks is during the Last Supper as recorded in John 14. Thomas asked the question, "Lord, we do not know where you are going. How can we know the way?" (v. 5) Because of his question, Jesus made this powerful, specific answer, "I am the way, and the truth, and the life. No one comes to the Father except through me" (v. 6).

"I am the way," the path.

"The truth," the truth; the true path.

"And the life." The truth gives believers strength to walk the path.

"No one comes to the Father except through me."

But all this was thrown out the back window when Jesus was crucified.

You will have times of courage. You will have times of belief. But this is what happens with disappointment—doubt settles in.

In Thomas you find doubt mixed with courage.

Remember the father who spoke to Jesus concerning his son whom the disciples could not cast out an evil spirit (Mark 9:24) "I believe; but help my unbelief."

"Help me. Help my unbelief." Something said in faith.

Thomas's doubt did not make Jesus reject him.

When Jesus died, Thomas struggled no more than the other disciples.

The third time Thomas spoke is recorded in John 20. Jesus had appeared to the other disciples, but Thomas was not present then. He refused to believe Jesus had risen from the dead without proof he could verify. He was quick to confess Jesus as Lord and God when that proof came.

Doubt should not be viewed as negative as long as it puts a hunger in your heart for truth.

No doubt exists that all these disciples changed after they grasped the power of the resurrection. It motivated them. It gave them power to go on. All the disciples were martyred, except John. And what of doubting Thomas? He spent the last eighteen years of his life in India where he was martyred for sharing the good news.

Thomas was transformed.

No matter how numb, hopeless, and full of doubt you may feel, it is no match for the power of the resurrection of Jesus Christ. Don't give up in the struggle. Don't give in to unbelief. Don't allow self to pull you down. Struggle to believe.

Let me tell you a story before going forward:

My great grandmother had a winter cellar for fruits and vegetables that she was not using anymore and thought it might be dangerous for the grandchildren. She asked me to break up the concrete on the top of the cellar and fill it in with dirt. So, I took my eight-pound sledgehammer and struck the concrete five times. I walked around the structure and thought about it, then struck the concrete five more times with the sledgehammer. I stood back, studied where I was hitting, and decided this was the best place to strike, then struck the concrete five more times.

Then Grandma came out and offered me some lemonade. I laid the sledgehammer down and drank some lemonade. It was just the thing I needed.

I walked over, picked up the sledgehammer, and began to strike with purpose. I was not going to give up until this was done. I struck four times, and it seemed it was denying me. I came down on the concrete in the same place as before and pushed through to the other side of the cellar. The whole thing caved in.

Five blows each time. Finally, the last fifth blow and the job was done.

Doubt seems like cured concrete. It just will not budge. I want you to consider five strikes that will burst doubt and drive you into the bedrock of faith.

⚠ Strike One: Face Your Doubts

Denying doubt drives it deeper toward unbelief.

At one church, I followed a pastor whose philosophy of problems was to overlook them, hoping they might go away. Realize that overlooked problems do not go away; they just grow and make more problems. When you ignore problems, you face bigger ones. If you want to be healthy in your relationships, your career, or your calling, face your problems.

If you want to remain healthy in your faith, face your doubts. Ask questions. Thomas was not afraid to ask questions, questions which brought about truth.

⚠ Strike Two: Face the Truth

Søren Kierkegaard made this observation about truth, "The truth is a snare: you cannot have it, without being caught. You cannot have the truth in such a way that you catch it, but only in such a way that it catches you." [32]

Have you allowed the truth of God's Word to catch you?

Jesus speaks of knowing the truth in John 8:31-32. "So Jesus said to the Jews who had believed him, 'If you abide in my word, you are truly my disciples, and you will know the truth, and the truth will set you free.'"

Do you want to be free, free from doubt, guilt, your past, worry, despair, habits? To be free, you must first come face-to-face with truth! To be free, you must know and trust the truth. Truth is an absolute. The world wishes to do away with absolutes. This is nothing new; It's been this way since the beginning. Ralph J. Cudworth, an English theologian and philosopher stated, "Truth is the most unbending and unpliable, the most necessary, firm, immutable, and unbreakable thing in the world."[33]

▲ Strike Three: Believe the Truth

Allow truth to become part of your belief system. Allow truth to redesign your map.

The world today accepts a truth that conforms to its belief system. In reality, truth nags at you. It will convict you. People do not want to be convicted of any wrongdoing or thinking, so they deny the truth. You may hear statements such as, "It's not my truth. It is yours."

Selwyn Duke wrote "The further a society drifts from Truth, the more it will hate those who speak it.""[34]

When people accept truth, they accept what truth proclaims, they receive what it says. As a believer, you must accept that God's Word is truth.

Consider the words of Jesus from His prayer in John 17.

"For I have given to them the words which You have given Me; and they have received them, and have known surely that I came forth from You; and they have believed that You sent Me" (v. 8).

"I have given them Your word; and the world has hated them because they are not of the world, just as I am not of the world" (v.14).

"Sanctify them by Your truth. Your word is truth" (v. 17).

To remain in the Word of God brings further transformation. To stray away from the Word of God allows bondage to make its way back into your life. Only the truth is able to crush that opposing, enslaving power and set you free.

To ban God's Word is to ban freedom. In truth, liberty is set before people.

The truth is that the blood of Christ:

- cleanses you from all sin
- keeps you from the punishment of sin
- gives you victory over the power of sin
- frees you from the fear of death.

This means you are free to live a life unchained, free to live a pure life, and free to make mistakes, learn from them, and move on to greater heights.

◢ STRIKE FOUR: APPLY THE TRUTH

Live it out! Applying truth drives it deeper into the bedrock of faith. It must be practiced to be of value.

A soap manufacturer, who was not a Christian, was walking one day with a minister. The soap maker said, "The Bible you preach has not done much good in the world. I see lots of wickedness and wicked people." Just then, they passed a child who was playing in the mud. He was very dirty.

The minister said, "Soap hasn't done much good in this world. I see lots of dirt and many dirty people."

"Oh," objected the soap maker, "You must remember that soap is useful only when it is applied."

"Exactly," answered the minister, "and so it is with the Word of God. It can help you only if you apply it."[35]

◢ STRIKE FIVE: SHARE THE TRUTH

You will find you cannot be silent.

As you speak the truth it drives belief deeper in your soul. It is developing a mindset.

You have to tell someone what Jesus has done for you.

Reflection

Which room are you in? The one full of doubts or the room in which Jesus has come? When the doubts fade, you will find Jesus was already in the room!

Is Jesus in your room?

Consider this warning from an anonymous writer. Your faith can move mountains and your doubt can create them.

Working under Jesus's authority you find confidence to journey to significance.

Milestone: Live Out Your Mission/Commission

ROADBLOCK: AIMLESSNESS

When I was in the military (Air Force, Strategic Air Command, 1968-1972), I read statistics about men who retired after serving in the military twenty to thirty years. It blew my mind how many (I do not remember the statistics) died after a couple of years following retirement. I began to ask men, "Who are you? What defines you?" Most of the answers were, "I am a (gives rank in the military)" or "I have this career." Their definition of themselves was found only in work they did or had retired from!

Aimless is defined as being without purpose or direction.

Synonyms for aimless include undirected, rudderless, adrift, and directionless.

I believe that finding who you are begins by defining whose you are. You are a child of God, a follower of Jesus Christ. Then you find your values.

What are your values? When you discover your values, you begin defining who you are. Your values define the who question of an individual, a church, or an organization.

I read a story of a eagle who grew up with chickens. "There is an old, well known story of a chicken farmer who found an eagle's egg. He put it with his chickens and soon the egg hatched. The young eagle grew up with all the other chickens and whatever they did, the eagle did too. He thought he was a chicken, just like them. Since the chickens could fly for a short distance, the eagle also learnt to fly a short distance. He thought that was what he was he was supposed to do. As a consequence, that was all he was able to do.

One cay the eable saw a bird flying high above him. He was very impressed. "Who is that?" he asked the hens around him. " That's the eagle, the king of birds," the hens told him. 'He belongs to the sky. We belong to the earth, we are just chickens."[36]

When you explore values, you are deciding what is at the core of who you are. The journey to find who you are begins with finding Christ, receiving Him as Savior and Lord . This answers the question of whose you are!

I believe values change when a person comes to Jesus, He does not just change a person's life, He transforms a person from the inside out.

Your values come out of your beliefs. Proverbs 23:7 states, "As he thinks in his heart, so is he" (NKJV). Beliefs are convictions or principles you know to be true.

What you believe really matters as your long-held deep beliefs develop your values. If you serve Satan, the world, or self, your values reflect who you serve. When you serve Jesus, your values reflect you serve Him.

When behavior matches values, you feel at peace with who you are, for you are more like yourself. When behavior does not match your values, you feel something is missing, you feel out of alignment. When the tires on your car are out of alignment, you can feel it in the steering wheel. When you are out of alignment with your values, you can feel it in the very core of your life.

Living your values builds integrity. Integrity is an architectural term meaning the state of being whole and undivided. A bridge that has integrity is safe to cross.

Proverbs 16:3 warns believers, "People may be pure in their own eyes, but the LORD examines their motives."

▲ REFLECTION

Do you know your values?

Are you in alignment with your values?

Living your values keeps you in alignment with who you are. It assures integrity!

Values define who you are. Mission defines what you do.

Jesus gave His followers their mission: make disciples. It is interesting that He did not say, "Stay and make disciples." He said. "Go, make disciples."

Jesus proclaimed this vision, "Go, make disciples of all nations."

Values define who you are. Mission defines what you do: make disciples. Vision directs where you go: to all nations (literally, ethnic groups). The vision is the transformation of all the world.

Values help to give personal direction. Roy Disney states, "When your values are clear to you, making decisions become easier."

Here are the values that guide my life.

1. Eternity. It is my firm belief in the end God has everything under control. Despite humanity's fall, God's plan will prevail. Working with my grandfather when I was a teenager, I often would make a mistake when helping him build a new house. He would look at my mistake, then look at me with a smile and say, "No one will know it one hundred years from now." He taught me to learn from my mistakes and to look forward into the future. He was giving me an eternal perspective, for which I am thankful.

2. Integrity. This has to do with keeping my alignment right. Proverbs 10:9 reminds me that "whoever walks

in integrity walks securely, but he who makes his ways crooked will be found out."

3. People. People are on the top of my task list. I include family under people. John 3:16 explains how much God values people.
4. Significance. Because I value people, I want to add value to people, to make a difference in their lives.
5. Discovery. I enjoy finding new ways to help develop people in training, mentoring, and speaking.
6. Growth. I found out if I grow, I can help others grow! To add value to others, I must grow.

Do you know your values? Share your values with someone close and ask how they see these values lived out in your lfie. If you cannot define your values to go https://www.gregwhite76.com/discover-your-values.html you will find a free download for discovering your values. Work through this download intentionally with much reflection. When you have discovered your values and written them down in a list go back over it and list your top five. Then think about how these values help define who you are and have become a guide for living. Share these with family members and friends and ask how they see these values live out in your life.

After you find who you are, then you define your mission. The purpose of a mission is to define what you do and guide you further in decision making.

Several years ago, I was attending a local Chamber of Commerce meeting. I asked our mayor, "What is the mission statement for our city, and vision?" I was told it was in a manual somewhere on a shelf in his office. Interesting. How can an organization find direction for what to do if the directions are on a shelf?

After working with a team and the city council for twelve months, the mission statement for the city was birthed for the city of Canton: "Partnering with our community to provide essential services, inspire citizens and strengthen our future."[37]

Without a mission statement, an organization is aimless. It does not know its purpose and wanders aimlessly, not knowing what to do.

This is where you find Jesus's disciples just after His death on the cross.

Roman guards were assigned to guard the tomb where Jesus was laid, signaling the disciples of Jesus to hide. The One who had taught them, the One who had showed the way, the One who had spoken words of life was dead. Their reason for being was laid on a shelf, sealed in a tomb. One word describes the disciples at this juncture in time: aimless. Life had lost its meaning.

How would you feel?

Do you feel that way now?

So many people today feel no reason for being and they wander in discontent, swallowed up in aimlessness. When there is no real purpose, people strike out against authority and join anything that sounds good to their ears and makes them feel good for the moment. You can observe an aimless society spiral downward day by day.

The first responsibility of a leader is to define reality, define the now, and see direction toward a preferred future. He must know where the team is before establishing where they are going. Then the leader must prepare people for the journey, get people on the bus and in the right seats before turning the key and shifting into forward.

Preparation is more than just knowing where the organization is going. It is knowing how you will get there, who is going with you, and preparing those who are going with you for the journey ahead. Think about this: the journey is more about who the group is becoming during the journey than the destination.

The struggle is in determining: Who am I? Why am I here? What am I to do? What is my purpose? What is my mission?

A mission or purpose statement not only states what you do, it also implies what you do not do. I believe the mission statement of an organization should be the litmus test for any new idea or venture.

My mission (the wording has improved over the years) is, "Guiding people to know and grow in a relationship with Jesus and one another."

My vision is to guide Pastors and church leaders to grow, navigate roadbocks, and celebrate milestones to make a difference in their calling.

Jesus's disciples were discouraged, feeling down after the Crucifixion. Their rabbi, their teacher, their leader, whom they put their trust for the future was dead and in a cold grave.

Suddenly, early Sunday morning, the stone closing the tomb was blown away. Light was seen coming out of darkness. Jesus appeared to the disciples several times. He addressed the aimlessness that was sure to vex His followers. "Go therefore and make disciples of all the nations, baptizing them in the name of the Father and of the Son and of the Holy Spirit, teaching them to observe all things that I have commanded you" (Matt 28:19–20a, NKJV). Interestingly, one of the last things Jesus gives His disciples is a mission.

So many people today do not know their mission in life.

Josh McDowell tells this story in *Stories from the Heart*.

An executive hirer, a "head-hunter" who goes out and hires corporate executives for other firms, once told me, "When I get an executive that I'm trying to hire for someone else, I like to disarm him. I offer him a drink, take my coat off, then my vest, undo my tie, throw up my feet and talk about baseball, football, family, whatever, until he's all relaxed. Then, when I think I've got him relaxed, I lean over, look him square in the eye and say, "What's your purpose in life?" It's amazing how top executives fall apart at that question."

"Well, I was interviewing this fellow the other day, had him all disarmed, with my feet up on his desk, talking about football, then I leaned up and said, "What's your purpose in life, Bob?" And he said, without blinking an eye, "To go to heaven, and take as many people with me as I can!" For the first time I was speechless. (Gray) [38]

I believe a mission statement for a church or an individual should address what Jesus has commissioned His followers to do: make disciples. A mission statement will affect many dimensions of a church or an individual.

Christlike character comes before the work of the mission. Galatians 5:22–23a helps to define what Christlike character is. "The fruit of the Spirit is love, joy, peace, longsuffering, kindness, goodness, faithfulness, gentleness, self-control" (NKJV).

I heard this story that highlights how being Christlike shows in your life.

Little Boy: "Mommy, my Sunday School teacher told me if I invite Jesus into my heart that He would come in there and live with me."

Mommy: "That's right, Honey. He will."

Little Boy: "But Mommy, won't a lot of Him stick out?"

That's a great definition of evangelism. A lot of Jesus sticks out of us.

Character is what sticks out. I opened up a training I was doing in a church on godly character with this statement: "God desires us to have character; He does not want us to be a character."

Vision determines where you go. "Go therefore and make disciples of all nations" (Matt 28:19, NKJV). Jesus did not say, "Come." He said, "Go." "Go" is a navigation term. "All nations" defines where and who. "Make disciples" identifies what. Too many times believers expect people to come to church to begin a relationship with Jesus. Jesus command believers to go to where people who need Him are.

When believers go, they are authorized by Jesus Christ. When believers go, all heaven has to offer is behind them. When believers go, Jesus is with them. Therefore go!

My vision: Helping pastor's and church leaders to grow in influence, navigate roadblocks, celebrate milestones, and make a difference in their calling.

III. Speaking: What you say and how you say it.

But sanctify the Lord God in your hearts, and always be ready to give a defense to everyone who asks you a reason for the hope that is in you, with meekness and fear" (1 Pet 3:15, NKJV).

Something is missing if others do not ask believers about their faith.

Someone has defined tact as "dealing with others as we would have them deal with us." The word comes from the Latin term *tactus* and means "to touch."

Believers must seek to touch the hearts of people, not knock them down with a club!

When I was at South Eastern Bible College (now Southeastern University), I traveled to Tampa on Saturdays with a group of friends and shared the good newswith people on the streets. I used to make a mark on an inside page of my Bible every time I prayed the sinner's prayer with someone. Then I came to realize that a conversation with someone about Christ was also very important, even if they did not want to pray the sinner's prayer at that time. Some plant. Some water. But God gives the increase (1 Cor 3:5–8).

A few years later I began to use a tweaked Engle's scale of conversion based on the work of James Engel to help me understand my role in the process of leading others to Christ.[39]

-6 Consciousness of God
-5 Contact with the gospel
-4 Considers the gospel
-3 Comprehends the gospel
-2 Conviction
-1 Choice
0 Conversion
+1 Change

Sometimes it takes a while to see someone go from one level to another.

Where on this scale are the people you are witnessing to, guiding to know Jesus?

What stragegy can you develop to take them to the next step toward choice?

Allow me to go back to the story I told of busting up concrete at my great grandmother's house. The first blow was as important as the last. Each blow weakened the structure and paved the way for the last blow to complete the mission.

You may be talking to someone about Christ whose heart is as hard as concrete. But with work of the Holy Spirit and the gentle persuasion of conversation, you or someone else will lead this person in the sinner's prayer. There will be great rejoicing in heaven. I believe the first conversation is as important as the last and each conversation leading to the last. Like a hammer, the Word of God may have to be applied often before it breaks the rock in pieces (Jer 23:29).

So do not stop witnessing. Be persistent! The next word or Scripture the person hears may be the final stroke that will open his or her heart to the gospel!

I believe bringing people to Christ is like picking apples. If the apple is not ripe, it hangs on the branch. If it is ripe, you can lift up the apple with the palm of your hand and it will let go. When you try to pull too hard, you push people away from Jesus.

Consider this quote by an atheist, Penn Jillette:

> How much do you have to hate somebody to not proselytize? How much do you have to hate somebody to believe that everlasting life is possible and not tell them that? I mean, if I believe, beyond a shadow of a doubt, that a truck was coming at you and you didn't believe it—that truck was bearing

down on you—there's a certain point where I tackle you, and this is more important than that.[40]

IV. Praying

"Continue earnestly in prayer, being vigilant in it with thanksgiving; meanwhile praying also for us, that God would open to us a door for the word, to speak the mystery of Christ, for which I am also in chains, that I may make it manifest, as I ought to speak" (Col 4:2–4, NKJV).

When you pray for someone to come to Christ, pray the Lord will send His Holy Spirit to convict that person and that his or her heart would be softened toward hearing the gospel. Pray that God would send other Christians to surround the person and be an influence for the Kingdom.

Do you have someone for whom you are praying to receive Christ? Pray again right now.

Believers are all called to fulfill the mission of making disciples.

Are you living out your mission?

What goals have you set that do not align to your mission?

You can make a difference in the lives of others through living out the mission Jesus has given to make disciples!

▲ THOUGHTS ABOUT PRESENTING VISION

Churches and businesses should have a mission statement and a vision statement to guide their work. A church or business leader is tasked with helping the organization to carry out the mission and fulfill the vision. One job of a leader is to get the staff on board with the vision and mission. Values are who you are. Mission is what you do. Strategy is how you carry out the mission. Vision is where you are going, and who is going with you.

How to Get People on the Bus and Influence People Who Want to Throw You Under The Bus

Nancy and I have served in churches where the word "one" did not come to our minds when describing those churches. They were divided in their thinking about the church. They had different ideas about what the church should be doing and how it should be done.

When a believer is walking in the flesh, he or she cannot walk in the Spirit. Those walking in the flesh who are influenced by the world instead of the Spirit cause division. They may sound spiritual and even act spiritual, but all the while they are hiding sins, usually gossip, pride, greed, or even lust. They desire to have a position because it gives them power. Influencing others would never enter their minds, but manipulation would. Have you met people like this?

⚜ FIRST STRIVE TO BECOME ONE IN THE SPIRIT

The Spirit making believers one does not mean that all believers see, feel, and or think the same way. It means they get along as brothers and sisters in Christ should. Differences should make believers stronger instead of divided. Pray that believers never see some things alike, for these differences of thought build creativity, which will give them an edge in the changing world.

Believers must be one in the mission of making disciples. Differences in thinking will help them tweak the vision to be more effective. This becomes real as believers are sensitive to the leading of the Holy Spirit.

Yet, some believers are not influenced by the Holy Spirit, but by mean-spiritedness. This hurts the Body and hinders the church from reaching out to others. I am tired of mean-spirited people controlling God's people.

To become one means believers get along, move forward

together, work together. They do not allow their differences to hinder the mission, but find ways to blend those differences to work together. They do not allow opinions to get out of hand, instead they choose to love each other deeply.

So how do you overcome issues in your own thinking and overcome being mean-spirited? Check your attitude. Not everyone will come aboard for your vision. Many will choose to wait and see. A few will jump on the bus and want it moving now. Watch your attitude with all these groups. The key is attitude, so check your own attitude. Remember, attitude is a choice!

▲ REFLECTION

How is your attitude toward a person who is mean-spirited?

Where are you allowing that person's attitude to overflow into your life?

How is your attitude affecting the rest of the church or your business?

Keep in mind that not everyone is going to jump on the band wagon of your ideas or the bus named vision. If ten percent run to the bus, another ten percent will try to throw you under the bus. More than eighty percent need clearer communication, especially the ten percent already on the bus.

Spend the majority of your time with fewer people. I cannot emphasize this enough. Develop, train, and encourage those already on the bus. Help this group influence others. This will be much more effective than doing it alone.

Last, but foremost, spend much time with God. R. T. Kendall writers, "I have discerned by trial and error that the more conscious I am of God's presence the more I feel like being myself. The less conscious I am of His presence the more I feel the need to prove myself. But the more I am myself the greater my liberty."[41] Become a person of presence by cultivating the presence of God in your life. People will not only see the difference, they will feel the difference in you. His presence transforms. Psalm 16:11 reminds you that in His presence "there is fullness of joy."

Too often people are content with the knowledge of God. Press on to experience God so your knowledge of Him moves from the head to the heart. When you enter God's presence with praise, He will enter your circumstances with power.

C. S. Lewis provided insights into experiencing the presence of God. "We may ignore, but we can nowhere evade the presence of God. The world is crowded with Him. He walks everywhere incognito."[42]

Do not lose sight of the truth that a moment in God's presence can change everything. Remember the words of Jesus, "Where your treasure is, there your heart will be also" (Matt 6:21).

⚜ REFLECTION

What is your purpose?

What is your mission?

Is there a sense of aimlessness that keeps you from moving forward with the mission?

Is the answer to "who am I" found in what you do or who you are in Christ?

A great resource to help you define who you are and begin the process of finding your purpose is Tom Wolfe's book, *Identity and Destiny: 7 Steps to a Purpose Filled Life.*

Another thing I would like to address at the end of this chapter is responsibility. A leader accepts responsibility, and the more responsibility you have, the less rights you have.

Consider the traditional pyramid structure used by many businesses today and how it may be reflected in your church. The pyramid speaks of climbing higher to reach the top and of rights instead of responsibility.

Consider another way to express structure:

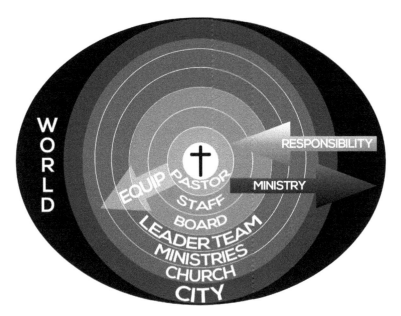

Concentric Circle Structure.

The concentric circle structure gives a different perspective to a church or organization. It represents people standing shoulder to shoulder to carry out the work of the mission. From this perspective the deeper one goes in the organization, the more responsibility. Responsibility is a better choice than power, because power in this context speaks of control and responsibility speaks of cooperation and collaboration. Thus, the deeper one goes, the more responsibility and wherever one is in the organization, ministry or serving goes outward. Remember the old adage fold your hands, "here is the church, here is the steeple, open the door and see all the people." The church is not the building, the church is people. Look at the chart below and see further differences between the pyramid model and the concentric circle model.

Pyramid Structure	Concentric Circle Structure
Command Base	Team Base
Individual	Group
Power	Empower
Control	Influence
My Idea	Our Idea
Rights	Responsibility
Climb	Serve

CHAPTER 6

Milestone: Companion

ROADBLOCK: UNHEALTHY RELATIONSHIPS

Paul gave this advice to the people of Corinth, "Do not be deceived: 'Bad company ruins good morals'" (1 Cor 15:33). Your friends influence you. Your relationships mold you.

To the church in Rome Paul wrote these timely words found in Romans 12:1–2:

> I appeal to you therefore, brothers, by the mercies of God, to present your bodies as a living sacrifice, holy and acceptable to God, which is your spiritual worship. Do not be conformed to this world, but be transformed by the renewal of your mind, that by testing you may discern what is the will of God, what is good and acceptable and perfect.

Corruption begins as you back away from God's Word and the influence of God's people. Your friends influence you to seek God or to distance yourself from Him.

Early in life I saw the influence of alcohol and drugs on my classmates, so I distanced myself from their influence. Some I wish I had stayed closer to, then maybe I could have influenced them.

Growing up in Russell Heights, I watched a man drink himself to death. He died of cirrhosis. He was one of the nicest men you would want to meet, until he was under the influence of alcohol. Then he was just mean. I saw a wonderful man with two sides because of this influence in his life. When I was twelve years old, I made a note to myself, *Drinking alcohol makes you stupid.* I know some will be upset with me because of this statement, but it was the observation of a twelve year old.

I have known people who could handle alcohol or some other substance for a while, but in the end it has a toll on people with its pull for more. Watch out, for bad company ruins good morals.

Who is influencing you? What is influencing you? Who are the people who encourage you in your walk with Jesus? Who are the people who discourage you and lead you away from Jesus?

Consider the words of Jesus as you think about the influencers in your life. "'This people honors me with their lips, but their heart is far from me; in vain do they worship me, teaching as doctrines the commandments of men'" (Matt 15:8–9). If your friends are influencing you to do anything unethical or to be immoral, you are hanging around with the wrong people.

I remember one time in the Air Force when I was stationed at Malmstrom AFB, Great Falls, Montana. One of men on the team offered me $50 to take a puff of a cigarette. I looked at him, smiled, and said, "No thanks." A few months later he received another assignment. He came to me before leaving and said, "Greg, I would have been very disappointed in you if you would have taken a drag on that cigarette."

His statement was an encouragement or an admonition for me to stay aligned with who I am—a child of God and a follower of Jesus Christ. This team member influenced me to make a difference.

Who are you influencing?

When people come to Jesus, His influence in their lives

overflows to influence their relationships. He transforms lives and encourages His followers.

Milestone: Companion

The Bible records multiple times God's promise to be with His people, to be a companion to them. Here are a few of those Scriptures.

"And the LORD appeared to him the same night and said, 'I am the God of Abraham your father. Fear not, for I am with you ... '" (Gen 26:24).

"God is our refuge and strength, a very present help in trouble" (Ps 46:1).

"Fear not, for I am with you; be not dismayed, for I am your God" (Isa 41:10).

"I am with you always, to the end of the age" (Matt 28:20b).

"And I will ask the Father, and he will give you another Helper, to be with you forever" (John 14:16).

The Greek word for helper in John 14:16 is *paraclete*. It means "someone who comes alongside to help." He is the One who is by your side. You can call on Him in every emergency.

Have you ever called on the Lord in an emergency? When I was sliding down the tube in a cave, I was calling on God for help! Many times I have called on the Lord during a time of danger and He helped me. Looking back, I wonder if God was saying, "Here he goes again. He really needs help this time."

When were times you called on the Lord when in danger? How can you use your experiences to encourage others to call on the Lord?

I have come to realize that calling on the Lord when I have been with Him earlier in the day is easier than when I have ignored Him. I have come to the awareness that He was there even before I called out to Him.

The Holy Spirit is your Helper who encourages you to continue. And as He encourages you, you are to encourage others. Paul reminded the believers in Thessalonica of how he had sent Timothy to strengthen and encourage them (1 Thess 3:2–3).

The translation of *paraclete* as "Comforter" came into English Bibles through Wycliffe's version (A.D. 1380) in the old sense of strengthener, from the Latin, *confortare*, which means "to strengthen much." The word Comforter meant "one who strengthens, invigorates." The Bible calls the Holy Spirit the Comforter because He encourages, exhorts, admonishes, protects, comforts, and guides Christians.

Paraclete is a difficult word to translate adequately. Estella Myers encountered that problem when translating the Bible for the people living in the Karre Mountains of Central African Republic. She was puzzled when her translation assistant commented, "If anyone would do all of that for us, we would say, 'He's the one who falls down beside us.'" The assistant went on to explain. When porters, carrying heavy loads on their heads, go on long journeys, they may become sick with malaria or dysentery, and in complete exhaustion may collapse along the trail. If a sick porter is left alone, he will be killed and eaten by wild animals during the night. If, however, someone sees him lying there and takes pity on him, picking him up and helping him to reach the safety of the next village, such a person is said to be "the one who falls down beside us." Such a person would be a comforter.[43]

Is the load too heavy? The Holy Spirit is by your side to give that extra lift. He comes by your side to help you.

Believers need a companion; they need the Holy Spirit. Listen to what Jesus said about Him in John 16, verses 7 and 13. "Nevertheless, I tell you the truth: it is to your advantage that I go away, for if I do not go away, the Helper will not come to you. But if I go, I will send him to you." "When the Spirit of truth comes, he will guide you into all the truth, for he will not speak on his own authority, but whatever he hears he will speak, and he will declare to you the things that are to come."

The Holy Spirit, the author of the Scriptures, is the illuminator and teacher of the Word. He will guide you into all truth. He makes truth real day by day, until you graduate and are fit for the more mature tasks of the school of faith. "But the Helper, the Holy Spirit, whom the Father will send in my name, he will teach you all things, and bring to your remembrance all that I have said to you" (John 14:26).

I have had high school and college students come to me and say, "Pastor, it is finals week. Pray with me that I pass the grade." I would respond by telling them that the Lord will help bring to their remembrance what they have studied. Then I ask them, "Have you studied for your finals?" Most will say they have. Some will look at me and say, "I have a lot of studying to do tonight."

Are you ready for your final exam?

Not only does the Holy Spirit teach you, He quickens your intellect to remember and learn. He is the author and the illuminator of the mind. He knows how to bring back forgotten truths in the moment of need.

He knows how to give the appropriate message for the fitting time, and then to bless it and send it home with lasting power. Trust Him to guide you, to speak through you, and to be your helper.

The Lord has spoken to me many times about how to respond to people to bring them to Jesus. One man would take his wife to church and drop her off in the parking lot. When I would see him, I would go to the car and say, "Richard, you don't have to sit in the car. You can come in the church with your wife." He responded in a way that told me he was a long way from knowing Jesus.

One day, I got a call. Richard has been told he has cancer. It was serious. I walked into his room in the hospital and shared with him my concern for him and asked him if I could pray with him. He looked up at me and said, "No."

I came back. He was beginning to warm up to me, instead of being so cold. I asked him if I could pray and he said, "Yes." I prayed for him, then began to talk to him about his relationship with Jesus. He said he didn't want to talk about that. So we changed the subject and talked for a while.

One day I walked into the hospital and began walking up the stairs. I stopped in an area between the floors and prayed, "Lord, You know Richard is on the edge of eternity and he needs You. Give me the right words to speak to him."

I walked into his room, pulled a chair by his bedside, looked him in the eyes, and said, "Richard, you know you are going to die soon. When you do, you are going to stand before God and give account for your life. What are you going to say to Him?" Richard looked at me and, with tears in his eyes, asked me to pray with him to ask Jesus in his heart. We prayed. The biggest smile came on his face and I could see a difference in his demeanor. His son called me later and said that his dad and him made amends.

The next Sunday was Easter. When I walked to the pulpit to preach, I spotted Richard sitting in a wheelchair in the back of the church with the biggest smile on his face. He had finally come to church because he had come to Jesus.

The next week Richard died. I buried a man who made the journey home to heaven. Some people you witness to through the years whose stories just stick with you. Richard's story is one for me. His story makes me remember I need the help of the Holy Spirit.

You carry with you the presence of the ones you spend the most time with. Who do you spend the most time with? Whose presence do you carry?

Jesus sent the Holy Spirit to come along side of believers to help them. He dwells within them to be their Companion.

Psalm 100 speaks loudly of the presence of God.

> Make a joyful shout to the LORD, all you lands! 2 Serve the LORD with gladness; Come before His presence with singing. 3 Know that the LORD, He is God; It is He who has made us, and not we

ourselves; We are His people and the sheep of His pasture. 4 Enter into His gates with thanksgiving, And into His courts with praise. Be thankful to Him, and bless His name. 5 For the LORD is good; His mercy is everlasting, And His truth endures to all generations.

Believers come to realize the manifest presence of the Lord through an ongoing relationship. They experience the presence of the Lord through daily times in prayer and by reading and applying His Word.

It's about connecting. Yet, some people who go to church say they have never felt the presence of God. Think about this: believers carry His presence with them as they encounter God throughout the day.

You carry with you the presence of those you spend the most time with. Everyone has presence. Everyone carries the influence of another. Whose presence do you carry?

You don't have to be around a person very long to become aware of his or her presence. That presence might be godly, influenced by God. It might be worldly, influenced by the world. It could be evil, influenced by Satan. It could even by selfish, influenced by self.

▲ PRESENCE

People have the ability to discern presence. When I am in a building alone and someone walks in, there are times I feel the person's presence before I see him or her. Is that strange? No. Haven't you ever felt someone is near and turned around to see someone? You were aware of another person invading your space, consciousness someone was near. God has built within people an awareness factor.

There are people who, when they walk into a room, you know it. You feel it. You sense a difference.

President Wilson used to tell a story about D. L. Moody. Wilson said he once went into a barber shop and took a chair next to the one in which D. L. Moody was sitting, though he did not know that Mr. Moody was there. He had not been in the chair very long before, as Wilson phrased it, he "knew there was a personality in the other chair." He began to listen to the conversation going on. He heard Mr. Moody tell the barber about the way of life. Wilson said, "I have never forgotten that scene to this day." When Mr. Moody was gone, Wilson asked the barber who the man was. When he was told it was D. L. Moody, President Wilson said: "It made an impression upon me I have not yet forgotten." [44]

Moody spent much of his time in the presence of Jesus. People carry presence.

What defines your presence?

At our first church I was preaching on forgiveness. A man stood up and began walking out of the service saying, "I will never forgive this man." He was carrying an attitude of unforgiveness, an attitude that had gripped his heart and moved him out of his seat.

I went to visit him that week. He asked my forgiveness and said he would be in church next week with a testimony. While driving home from the service, God had convicted him. He forgave the man who stole his business and thousands of dollars. It was a difficult choice for him to make, yet he knew if he kept this attitude of unforgiveness, it would affect others. So he forgave.

Who do you need to forgive?

He stood up next week and asked the church to forgive him. He was a board member of the church. His wisdom in certain matters was helpful to me and our church.

What defines the presence you carry?

God created people to be aware and to respond to the world

around them. Humans are tripartite (three parts): body, soul, and spirit (1 Thes 5:23). The body responds to the physical world. The soul responds to the intellectual and logical. Even emotional input is translated from what is sensed through seeing, hearing, smell, touch, and taste. The spirit responds to the spiritual. People sense the presence of the Lord. Responses are influenced by what people have known or experienced in the past.

As followers of Jesus, believers are people of presence. They know what it is to be aware of God's manifest presence. As they enter God's presence, change will be observed in their lives.

You can change the nature of your presence by choosing to ask God to renew a right spirit within you (Ps 51:10). It is intentional. Attitude is a choice. But until the pain of remaining the same hurts more than the pain of change, you will prefer to stay where you are and allow others to grow beyond you.

When people allow God to transform them, they grow. I remember a man who would tell me that all change is bad. His attitude told me he preferred to stay the same.

You must make sacrifices to go deeper into the presence of the Lord. You can change your nature, attitude, and the presence you carry by choice. You can't control your circumstances, but you can control your attitude. Your attitude projects presence.

When you enter God's presence with praise, He will enter your circumstances with power. The account of Paul and Silas praising God in jail is an outstanding example of this.

Understand that worship moves you into the presence of the Lord. Psalm 22:3 states that God inhabits the praises of His people.

Realize that His presence adjusts your attitude. Often times when you are down, you are being self-centered. Praise and worship direct your attention beyond yourself, your problems, and your fears to God and His goodness to you. Proverbs 17:22 points out that a "cheerful heart is good medicine, but a crushed spirit dries up the bones" (NIV).

Appreciate that His presence creates opportunities to witness. Those who face adversity, who are praising God and being thankful, have the undivided attention of those who have not yet found the source of such strength. Again, think of the account found in Acts 16 of Paul and Silas in jail. They are singing and praising God. Then comes an earthquake. This leads the jailer to come to faith in the Lord. Praise turns a prison into a sanctuary.

Paul and Silas could have walked out. The other prisoners could have walked out. But the presence of God kept them there. You don't want to walk away from the manifest presence of God.

A moment in God's presence changes everything. This is why the Psalmist could sing, "In your presence there is fullness of joy" (Ps 16:11). His presence in your life makes a difference, developing within you the ability to make a difference in other people's lives. This is significance.

CHAPTER 7

Milestone: Live Out Your Calling

ROADBLOCK: DISCOURAGEMENT/FRUSTRATION

What frustrations do you face in ministry or in the work you do?

Are you discouraged in your calling?

All people face discouragement from time to time. When serving at the first church I pastored, I wrote out a resignation letter every Monday morning and put it on my desk. By Monday afternoon I knew I could not resign from the call God had given me.

You can resign a job. You can change your career. But you cannot give up your call. You can run from it, but it will catch you and pull you back in the game.

I remember speaking at a church in which someone came to me after the sermon and said he had left the ministry. He was miserable. Nancy and I drove home that night in silence. We decided not to become like that. We will stay in the call.

Sometimes frustrations are an indication of your calling. I have faced frustrations through the years while pastoring. Most of my frustrations were with people not growing in the Lord. I believe when people come to Christ, the Holy Spirit immediately begins to work with them to become more like Jesus.

Now you may ask, "Greg, have you arrived." I will tell you immediately, "No". My wife and those who know me best would agree. Yet, a transformation is happening in me and in everyone who follows Jesus. Think about this. Look at the bottom of your feet. If there is no gold dust on your soles, then you are not in heaven. While you are here on this earth, you will struggle to become what God wants you to be. That struggle is called sanctification.

My gift of the Spirit from Romans 12 is exhortation. When I started in ministry, my gift was prophecy, the opposite of mercy. People prayed I would change. A few years passed and I came to grips with my calling more clearly. God helped me change to be used in the gift of exhortation. That is, God enables me to stimulate faith and encourage growth in others. I emphasize practical application, being insistence on outward proof of inner convictions through encouraging a person to pursue a specific course of conduct.

Frustrations will either take you toward depression and anger or they will guide you to realize your calling and stay on track. You overcome frustrations by coming to God, asking for His help and for insight into what He is teaching you. Looking back, my greatest times of frustration became my turning points to greater personal growth and growth in the congregation I was pastoring.

Your calling is bigger than you.

Several of the disciples had a career as fishermen! One day Jesus came and stood near their boats. Mark's Gospel records when Jesus called two of them to follow Him. "Passing alongside the Sea of Galilee, he saw Simon and Andrew the brother of Simon casting a net into the sea, for they were fishermen. And Jesus said to them, 'Follow me, and I will make you become fishers of men.' And immediately they left their nets and followed him (Mark 1:16–18).

When you have a calling, your calling goes beyond you. It is not about you; it is through you to others. Think about it this way, "I was created for something beyond myself."

A calling doesn't originate with you, but is an upward call. God calls you to something bigger than yourself. And when God calls you, He equips you to fulfill the call.

God called me to be a pastor. Yet I had flunked speech class twice because I could not speak in front of the class. I argued with God about this. "Lord, I flunked speech class!. How can I walk up in front of people and preach Your Word?" Looking back, I realize God smiled.

During my time of ministry, I have preached and given speeches more than six thousand times. I am still learning how to improve by taking classes, having a mentor, and reflecting after speaking. I figure someday I can be a great speaker.

My calling is to be a pastor. I believe the scope of my calling goes beyond pastoring a church to pastoring the community.

I have learned about calling from one of my mentors, John Maxwell. You work a job. You build a career. You fulfill your calling.

I believe God has called believers to something bigger than themselves. You may have a job. You may be building a career. But God has called you to something bigger than yourself. It may be your career is key to your calling. God is strategically placing you in a community to make disciples. You will make a difference. If you discover and fulfill your call, you will feel fulfilled and find significance, because you will have developed character and abilities to make a difference in others.

Renew your call.

There are times when you are discouraged and frustrated. You need to spend more time with Jesus to renew His call again.

Consider the story of the Apostle Peter recorded in John 21:1–19. Just a few days before, Peter denied Jesus three times. He had not been a rock. (Peter means rock.) After His resurrection, Jesus appeared to Simon Peter to renew his calling. Three times Jesus addresses him as Simon, son of John. Simon was a reed blown by the wind in different directions. With this renewed call, Simon again becomes the rock Jesus saw in him when he was first called.

▲ Reflection

When are there times the old ways show up?
What triggers pull you away from your calling?
What Scriptures can you use to keep you on track?
Who can speak to you when you are heading off track?

Keep in tune with your call.

You come face-to-face with the great decision when you hear Jesus speak these words, "If anyone would come after me, let him deny himself and take up his cross and follow me" (Mark 8:34). Following Jesus is an individual commitment. You must come. Action is required on your part. You must do something. Coming to Jesus is personal. You must do it alone. "Come" is a personal invitation. It is intimate. It is you and Jesus.

The hardest thing to do is not to take up your cross, but to deny self. When you come to Jesus, receive Him into your life, you begin a journey of following Him. Focusing on following Him is denying yourself.

Your career is you. Your calling is bigger than you. And God, who calls you, is bigger still. It's not about you. Your calling fulfills you, yet you may never fulfill your calling.

▲ Reflection

What is your calling?

Do you have the same passion for the call as when you first discovered your passion?

Consider the warning of Jesus to believers found in Revelation 2:4–5. "But I have this against you, that you have abandoned the love you had at first. Remember therefore from where you have fallen; repent, and do the works you did at first. If not, I will come to you and remove your lampstand from its place, unless you repent."

Do you need to renew your passion for what God has called you to?

To renew your passion and renew your calling, spend quality time inspecting yourself and asking God to help you keep in tune with your call.

There is a story of a shepherd who called in from an isolated place and asked a radio announcer to play a certain key on the radio so he could tune his guitar.

Have breakfast with Jesus and renew your call, you will keep your calling "in tune."

Call a friend and talk it over with him or her. Pray. Keep praying until you renew your call.

Then you will find fulfillment instead of discouragement. You will find fulfillment in overcoming, recommitting to your call and staying in the journey.

Paul wrote of staying focused on his call in Philippians 3:12–14.

> "Not that I have already attained, or am already perfected; but I press on, that I may lay hold of that for which Christ Jesus has also laid hold of me. Brethren, I do not count myself to have apprehended; but one thing I do, forgetting those things which are behind and reaching forward to those things which are ahead, I press toward the goal for the prize of the upward call of God in Christ Jesus."

What do you need to do to reach the prize of the upward call?

Think about your calling as you read the verses below:

"I, therefore, the prisoner of the Lord, beseech you to walk worthy of the calling with which you were called" (Eph 4:1, NKJV).

How can you "walk worthy of the calling...?"

Where are you intentional in finding encouragement as you continue your calling?

"To this end we always pray for you, that our God may make you worthy of his calling and may fulfill every resolve for good and every work of faith by his power, so that the name of our Lord Jesus may be glorified in you, and you in him, according to the grace of our God and the Lord Jesus Christ" (2 Thes 1:11–12).

When you are discouraged in your calling (discouragement will come), you can find encouragement by going back to the One who called you. Talk to God about your discouragement and frustrations. You will discover God is there to help you and give further direction. And you will "fulfill every resolve for good and every work of faith *by His power.*"

Be intentional in your calling and you will make a difference.

CHAPTER 8

Milestone: Daily Fill to Capacity

ROADBLOCK: POWERLESS

Countless stories can be found of men and women in ministry facing burnout and depression. Many reasons for this could be cited, but one major reason is a lack of leaning on God, i.e., being in His presence and finding the strength and capacity to carry on the work God has called you to do.

Believers can do the Lord's work in their own strength, though it will not be most effective. Believers can do the work of the Lord, yet forget to seek the Him and His help in ministry.

I remember a time I went to visit a man who was in depression. As I sat outside his house in my car, I began to cry. I looked at the house. But I just could not get out of the car to encourage someone because I lacked the power to do it. I started the car, drove past my office directly to my home and sat in my living room helpless.

The next day I was sitting in my office when Deborah Wallace, a Christian counselor who had an office down from mine, stepped into my office and shared with me that I was facing depression. She suggested I see a doctor and come visit her office in an official capacity for counseling. I saw that doctor who put me on depression medicine. Then I went through several weeks of counseling.

One day I had an epiphany as I realize the real problem—I was dry spiritually. Depression literally siphons the life out of you, leaving little capacity or ability for adding value to others. I was not spending time with God. I was doing God's work without Him. I began an intentional regiment of seeking God and reading His Word. I realized that not only did I have a chemical imbalance, I had a spiritual imbalance that was impeding my ministry to people. When you forget to keep your devotional life strong, you face spiritual depression. I needed a fresh relationship with God.

Paul gave this instruction and admonition to the church at Ephesus. "And do not get drunk with wine, for that is debauchery, but be filled with the Spirit (Eph 5:18). The first part of this verse was not a problem I ever faced. But the second part was one I faced. I got alone and sought the Lord for a refilling of His Spirit. Then I realized that not only was I facing a physical battle, but I was also facing a greater spiritual battle. That awareness helped me look at the problem differently. Did I need the depression medicine? At the time, yes! But I needed something greater, a fresh revelation of God's presence in my life. The greatest difference was made by a refilling of God's Spirit. A woman commented to D. L. Moody of her husband, "Don't fill him, he leaks." The same could be said of me. The reality is all believers leak and all need a fresh move of God in their lives.

Realize that when God is about to do a great thing, He chooses a person to do His work.

God chose a man, literally homeless for a time, to lead His people out of Egypt. Moses grew up with Egypt's royal family. Yet because he took the side of his own people, the Israelites, he fled Egypt and wandered through the wilderness for forty years, becoming a shepherd of another man's flock. But God did not forget him. God appeared to Moses in a burning bush and called him to lead His people. Exodus 3:1–2 was a passage I chose early in ministry to remind me of what God had called me to do.

"Now Moses was keeping the flock of his father-in-law, Jethro, the priest of Midian, and he led his flock to the west side of the wilderness and came to Horeb, the mountain of God. And the angel of the Lord appeared to him in a flame of fire out of the midst of a bush. He looked, and behold, the bush was burning, yet it was not consumed."

Moses's story spoke to me of my responsibility to keep the flock and lead it through the wilderness (this world) to the mountain of God. The responsibility of leaders is to lead God's people to Him, to bring His people into His presence. To do that, leaders must themselves be in God's presence. They must be people of Presence.

The story of the Exodus is the story of a man leading God's people out of Egypt. It was evident that Moses had been with God, otherwise he could not have done it.

Since change often comes at a quick pace, leaders must be principle driven. Methods are many, Principles are few. Methods always change, Principles never do.

Here is one principle spiritual leaders must always pursue. "But you shall receive power when the Holy Spirit has come upon you; and you shall be witnesses to Me in Jerusalem, and in all Judea and Samaria, and to the end of the earth" (Acts 1:8, NKJV). Leaders need His power because they cannot do the work of the ministry alone. They must work in the power of the Holy Spirit.

▲ THE HOLY SPIRIT GIVES BELIEVERS POWER

Think about this statement as you read the definitions below.
Power (pou^{1}er) n.

1. The ability or capacity to perform or act effectively.
2. Strength or force exerted or capable of being exerted; might. See synonyms at strength.

3. The ability or official capacity to exercise control; authority.

Capacity (ke-pàs¹î-tê) n.

1. The ability to receive, hold, or absorb.
2. Ability to perform or produce; capability.
3. The power to learn or retain knowledge; mental ability.
4. Innate potential for growth, development, or accomplishment; faculty.

Acts 1:8 is speaking of the baptism in the Holy Spirit. God is giving believers the ability—the capacity—to be witnesses. The purpose of the baptism in the Holy Spirit is power, the capacity or ability to witness and to carry out the Great Commission.

All believers are entitled to, and so should ardently expect and earnestly seek, the promise of the Father, the baptism in the Holy Spirit, according to the command of the Lord Jesus Christ. This was the normal experience of all believers in the early Christian church. With it comes the enduement of power for godly living and service through the bestowment of the gifts and their uses in the work of the ministry ((Luke 24:49; Acts 1:4, 8; 1 Cor 12:1–31). This experience is distinct from and subsequent to the experience of the new birth (Acts 8:12–17; 10:44–46; 11:14–16; 15:7–9).[45]

It is important to understand what the baptism in the Holy Spirit is. R. A. Torrey provides three statements that bring clarification.

1. The baptism with the Holy Spirit is a definite experience.[46]

Jesus commanded His followers in Luke 24:49, "I am sending the promise of my Father upon you. But stay in the city until you are clothed with power from on high." On the Day of Pentecost, when the Spirit was poured out, the disciples did not look at each other with questions or have long debates whether or not they had received that promise. They knew!

If it was not a definite experience, how could they tarry until it happened?

Have you asked Jesus to baptize you in the Holy Spirit?

2. The baptism with the Holy Spirit is a work of the Holy Spirit distinct from and additional to His regenerating work.[47]

At salvation, the Holy Spirit baptizes the believer into the body of Christ, according to 1 Corinthians 12:13. "For in one Spirit we were all baptized into one body." At the baptism in the Holy Spirit, Christ baptizes believers in the Spirit. Matthew 3:11 records John the Baptist's statement that Jesus would " baptize you with the Holy Spirit and fire."

The baptism in the Holy Spirit is not salvation, but an experience clearly shown as the fulfillment of the promise made to those who believe. "And Peter said to them, "Repent and be baptized every one of you in the name of Jesus Christ for the forgiveness of your sins, and you will receive the gift of the Holy Spirit. For the promise is for you and for your children and for all who are far off, everyone whom the Lord our God calls to himself" (Acts 2:38–39).

3. The baptism with the Holy Spirit is a work of the Holy Spirit always connected with and primarily for the purpose of testimony and service.[48]

Jesus has already commissioned the apostles. He has been with them three years. They witnessed His death, resurrection, and were about to witness His ascension. So why did He command them to wait? Because the Spirit's work in believers relates to their testimony and service.

When faced with persecution, the disciples sought the Lord. "They were all filled with the Holy Spirit and continued to speak the word of God with boldness" (Acts 4:31b).

In Old Testament times, the Spirit worked in God's people so they could serve Him. Moses and the seventy elders are but one example of this (Numbers 11:16–17).

Even Jesus did not begin His ministry until being filled with the Spirit of the Lord. "Then Jesus, being filled with the Holy Spirit, returned from the Jordan and was led by the Spirit into the wilderness" (Luke 4:1, NKJV). If Jesus, when He ministered on earth needed to be filled with the Holy Spirit, I believe His followers need that experience also.

Believers need the Holy Spirit to do God's work.

Jesus loved His disciples and would have loved to continue with them. Yet He told them, "It is to your advantage that I go away" (John 16:7). Why? Because if He left He would send the Holy Spirit to them. The baptism in the Holy Spirit is for the empowerment of believers for service, witness, spiritual warfare, and boldness in their testimonies (Acts 1:8; 4:19–20, 29–31; 6:8–10; 1 Cor 2:4). Jesus wanted His disciples to be full of the Holy Spirit.

Evangelist Mike Livengood shares three reasons why Jesus wants you to be baptized in the Holy Spirit.

1. You need a comforter (John 14, 16). People living in stress need a comforter.
2. You need a teacher. Since the Holy Spirit is the author of God's Word, it is to your advantage to know the Author to preach and teach it.
3. You need power.

A man had a factory. He walked around the outside and then walked around the inside. There were shafts, all properly set, the cogs, all sharp and clean, the great engine all complete.

The machinery was all there, but it did not move a spoke. He was looking disgustedly at the factory when a man came up and asked, "Your factory?"

"Yes"

"What do you make?"

"That's the trouble. I don't make anything.

"Doesn't it run?"

"No!"

"What's the matter with it?"

"I don't know!"

"Ah," said the man, "I'll tell you. You need to get some hook-nosed oil cans and some imported oil."

So he employed some men to go around and oil the machinery and all the bearings. Then he came again, walking inside and outside. Nothing moved.

Another man came up to him and asked, "Your factory?"

"Yes," he replied.

What do you make?"

"Don't make anything."

"Don't it run?"

"No."

"What's the matter?"

"I don't know."

"I'll tell you. You want to fresco it on the side walls and ceiling. I would recommend you put a couple of barefooted angels with trumpets eternally ready to blow—and do it properly."

So he brought workmen in and frescoed the factory, putting a couple of angels on the ceiling with trumpets at their lips, ready to blow. Then he came down and looked it over again. But still it did not move.

While he was looking a third man came up to him and asked, "Your factory?"

"Yes," he replied.

"What do you make?"

"Don't make anything."

"Don't it run?"

"No."

"What's the matter?"

"Don't know."

"Ah," he said, "I'll tell you. It has no steeple. You want to put up a nice steeple on one of the corners. And I'd advise you to put in a fine pipe organ. And get a choir at the same time."

So he set men to work who got the steeple up, with a chime of bells that was marvelous. They put in a pipe organ and got a choir that would beat anything you ever heard, especially on the "amen." Then the man came down, saw the steeple and the organ and heard the choir and the chimes. But not a thing moved.

"This your factory?" asked a man who came up to him.

"Yes," he replied.

"What do you make?"

"Don't make anything."

"Don't it run?"

"No."

"What's the matter?"

"I don't know."

"Ah," he said, "you want a picture of the thing taken. Get a photographer to take a picture. Have a lot of copies made and framed and hung all round in the railway stations, hotels, barber shops, and so on, telling people it will move at 10:30 in the morning and 6:00 at night. Then people will come to see it move."

So he got a picture taken and had copies hung up at all the places the man told him about. Then he came down, walked around inside and out, but couldn't see anything moving. He was perfectly disgusted. Not a cog trembled.

Just then a working man came up, a hard-handed man. He took off his hat. He was very polite and asked, "Beg pardon, sir. Is this your factory?"

"Who told you to ask me that? grunted the owner.

"Beg pardon, but is that your factory?" repeated the man.
"Yes."

"What do you make?"

"Don't make anything?"

"Don't it run?"

"Run! No, it doesn't run at all, except into debt."

"What's the matter, sir?"

"I don't know. A man told me to get some hook-nosed oil cans—and there they are. Another man told me to fresco it and put in a couple of angels. I frescoed it and, if you will come in and have a look, you will see two bare footed angels on the ceiling ready to blow their trumpets. Another man told me to put on a steeple, to get a pipe organ, to engage a choir, and I did. Do you hear those chimes? See the organ? Listen to the choir chasing that "amen" up and down! Another man told me to get a photograph taken and hung up. I have hung it up! But the machinery doesn't move a spoke. I am disgusted with the whole business."

"Well," said the working man, "Pardon me, sir. I have never been to school and I don't know anything about those angels, but I would like to ask one question: Did you ever put fire in the boiler?"

"Why, I never thought of that."

"Well," said the working man, "if you will take the chance, it will scare the choir, likely. I will put some fire in the boiler."

"Oh," said the man, "go ahead. Move it somehow. Make something of it, if it's only ashes."

So, the working man went inside, took off his coat, opened the door of the furnace, put in the wood, threw on the petroleum, put in the coal, lit a match, got the fire going, set on the draughts, shoveled in some more coal, and pulled back the throttle valves. The steam rushed to the cylinder, hit the end of the piston rod. The great wheel began to tremble. It revolved, and the machinery all over the factory began to move. He added a little more coal, and more and more and more. Faster and faster and faster went the machinery. The choir got scared and went out the back door. The whole machinery was moving.[49]

What is most needed in the church? Is it the fresco? No! Is it the choir? No! Is it the stained glass windows? No! Is it the advertisements? No! Is it the power of the Spirit? Yes!

Be intentional in your calling and you will make a difference.

Think about this quote from Bill Easum, «We live in a secular world, but the church continues to develop ministries as if the church were in charge of a Christian Society."[50]

What does this quote say about the church today?

What does this say about the need to rely on God and be filled with the Holy Spirit?

Emotion is good. Power is better—power to be a witness.

Are you getting filled daily? It will change your life!

Do you feel a lack of power in your life?

Do you have a hunger for more of God? As you seek God and press in for more, He answers your prayer.

▲ SERVE: POWER TO WITNESS BY YOUR WORKS

The baptism in the Holy Spirit is for empowerment for service!

Read Luke 4:14–21 and see the connection of the Holy Spirit in Jesus's ministry on earth.

> And Jesus returned in the power of the Spirit to Galilee, and a report about him went out through all the surrounding country. 15 And he taught in their synagogues, being glorified by all.
>
> 16 And he came to Nazareth, where he had been brought up. And as was his custom, he went to the synagogue on the Sabbath day, and he stood up to read. 17 And the scroll of the prophet

Isaiah was given to him. He unrolled the scroll and found the place where it was written,

18 "The Spirit of the Lord is upon me, because he has anointed me to proclaim good news to the poor. He has sent me to proclaim liberty to the captives and recovering of sight to the blind, to set at liberty those who are oppressed, 19 to proclaim the year of the Lord's favor."

20 And he rolled up the scroll and gave it back to the attendant and sat down. And the eyes of all in the synagogue were fixed on him. 21 And he began to say to them, "Today this Scripture has been fulfilled in your hearing."

If Jesus did His ministry in the power of the Spirit, should you not desire that same power to assist you in ministry? If Jesus did not begin ministry until He became endued from on high, you must not begin ministry until you have been endued from on high.

Listen to Jesus's instruction to His disciples concerning the promise of the Father, which is the baptism in the Holy Spirit.

45 Then he opened their minds to understand the Scriptures, 46 and said to them, "Thus it is written, that the Christ should suffer and on the third day rise from the dead, 47 and that repentance for the forgiveness of sins should be proclaimed in his name to all nations, beginning from Jerusalem. 48 You are witnesses of these things. 49 And behold, I am sending the promise of my Father upon you. But stay in the city until you are clothed with power from on high" (Luke 24:45–49).

The baptism of the Holy Spirit is an absolute necessity in every Christian's life for the service to which God has called them.

⚜ SPEAK: POWER TO WITNESS BY YOUR WORDS

Jesus spoke of how the power of the Spirit would enable believers to witness by their words. "'When the Spirit of truth comes, he will guide you into all the truth, for he will not speak on his own authority, but whatever he hears he will speak, and he will declare to you the things that are to come. 14 He will glorify me, for he will take what is mine and declare it to you'" (John 16:13–14).

In the Book of Acts you find several examples of the empowering by the Spirit. Three of those accounts are provided below.

> But when they had commanded them to leave the council, they conferred with one another, 16 saying, "What shall we do with these men? For that a notable sign has been performed through them is evident to all the inhabitants of Jerusalem, and we cannot deny it. 17 But in order that it may spread no further among the people, let us warn them to speak no more to anyone in this name." 18 So they called them and charged them not to speak or teach at all in the name of Jesus. 19 But Peter and John answered them, "Whether it is right in the sight of God to listen to you rather than to God, you must judge, 20 for we cannot but speak of what we have seen and heard" (Acts 4:15–20).

> "And now, Lord, look upon their threats and grant to your servants to continue to speak your word with all boldness, 30 while you stretch out your hand to heal, and signs and wonders are performed through the name of your holy servant Jesus." 31 And when they had prayed, the place in which they were gathered together was shaken,

and they were all filled with the Holy Spirit and continued to speak the word of God with boldness (Acts 4:29–31).

And Stephen, full of grace and power, was doing great wonders and signs among the people. 9 Then some of those who belonged to the synagogue of the Freedmen (as it was called), and of the Cyrenians, and of the Alexandrians, and of those from Cilicia and Asia, rose up and disputed with Stephen. 10 But they could not withstand the wisdom and the Spirit with which he was speaking (Acts 6:8–10).

Let me ask you two vital questions about your Christian life. Have you been baptized in the Holy Spirit? If not, you need to receive this Baptism! Are you using His power in daily living? If not, you need a refilling!

I was listing to a sermon years ago, I do not remember the speaker, he gave this illustration of needing to be refilled. D L Moody was giving a challenge after his sermon on the baptism of the Holy Sprit and as a man rose from his chair to respond to the challenge, his wife yelled out, 'Don't do it Mr. Moody, he leaks." Well the truth is we all "leak" I have noticed it in my life, I need a refilling daily. Why is it so necessary, consider a verse which speaks of our need for strength from the Lord? Think about it we all become exhausted from time to time.

> Have you not known? Have you not heard? The LORD is the everlasting God, the Creator of the ends of the earth. He does not faint or grow weary; his understanding is unsearchable. 29 He gives power to the faint, and to him who has no might he increases strength. 30 Even youths shall faint and be weary, and young men shall fall exhausted;

> 31 but they who wait for the LORD shall renew
> their strength; they shall mount up with wings
> like eagles; they shall run and not be weary; they
> shall walk and not faint (Isaiah 40:28–31).

Fred Smith reminds believers that power must be partnered with humility. "Humility is not denying the power you have. It is realizing that the power comes through you, not from you."[51] When we believe the power or strength comes from within ourselves this is where we struggle with exhaustion that produces discouragement and or frustration. It is through humility we overcome pride and realize our strength is not from within ourselves and we seek God for the power, the strength we need.

As I wrote this book I wanted to speak to Christians of many denominations, not just my own.

Please allow me to speak plainly to those who call themselves pentecostal, I am fifth generation Assembly of God. Luke expresses the words of Jesus regarding the baptism into the Holy Spirit clearly describing purpose: "But you shall receive power when the Holy Spirit has come upon you; and *you shall be witnesses* to Me in Jerusalem, and in all Judea and Samaria, and to the end of the earth" (Acts 1:8, NKJV).

As Pentecostals we can say we have the power but we can come to the place we worship the power and not practice the power in our lives. The purpose of the baptism into the Holy Spirit is to give power to guide people to know Jesus and grow in their relationship with Jesus so that they become more like Him. To practice the power of the Holy Spirit in our lives is to be a catelyst of change not only in the lives others, but in our own lives first.

Through the Pentecostal experience of being filled with the Spirit, God is preparing believers to make disciples by sharing Jesus's story to a lost generation. Immediately following the Day of Pentecost you see a difference in Jesus's disciples.

1. They expressed concern and compassion to others.
2. They found courage to face problems in their lives and the lives of others.
3. They displayed calm and peace in a time of uncertainty.
4. They ministered to people with confidence using their God-given authority.
5. They followed His command to make disciples
6. People became aware they live in the presence of the Holy Spirit.
7. They were living within their gifts and calling.
8. They expressed confidence and displayed power in their words and actions.
9. They made a difference in the lives of others.[52]

I believe you may find the Book of Acts continues being written in the journals of heaven and in the lives of people today. Is your name written in these journals? You can make a difference in the lives of others through the power of the Holy Spirit

CHAPTER 9

Significance

Significance is not a chapter in your life, which you write and go on to the next. Significance is woven daily in your story as you add value to other people. It is a choice. You choose significance. It is woven tighter into the fabric of your life every time you choose to make a difference in the lives of others.

First Thessalonians 5:11 instructs believers, "Therefore encourage one another and build up one another, just as you are doing." Encouraging one another points to adding value to one another. Encouragement has many facets.

🔺 ENCOURAGING OTHERS HELPS KEEP YOU ON COURSE

A pilot friend of mine, John Cosmos, teaches that if a plane is off course by one degree for sixty miles it is 1 mile off course. At times, you must stop to take your bearings to make sure you are on the right course.

From time to time in your Christian walk you can get off course and need assistance getting back on course. The Apostle Paul felt confidence in the ability of believers to help one another do this by admonishing one another (Rom 15:14). Admonish here means to put in mind, to caution or reprove gently, to warn. Paul instructed believers in Thessalonica to gently reprove disorderly brothers and sisters to get them back on course in 2 Thessalonians 3:11–15.

> For we hear that some among you walk in idleness, not busy at work, but busybodies. 12 Now such persons we command and encourage in the Lord Jesus Christ to do their work quietly and to earn their own living.13 As for you, brothers, do not grow weary in doing good. 14 If anyone does not obey what we say in this letter, take note of that person, and have nothing to do with him, that he may be ashamed. 15 Do not regard him as an enemy, but warn him as a brother.

Sometimes believers tend to miss one part of encouragement may be to admonish or "warn him as a brother," or a sister. This may be because one must "take note of that person" to admonish.

Galatians 6:1 provides guidance in encouraging others. "Brothers, if anyone is caught in any transgression, you who are spiritual should restore him in a spirit of gentleness. Keep watch on yourself, lest you too be tempted." Restoration is yet another way to encourage people to stay on course and keep on the journey.

Leonardo Da Vinci reminds us, "An arch consists of two weaknesses when leaning against one another makes a strength."[53]

"Let the word of Christ dwell in you richly, teaching and admonishing one another in all wisdom, singing psalms and hymns and spiritual songs, with thankfulness in your hearts to God" (Col 3:16). Music lifts the soul. Something about singing or even humming praise songs to the Lord encourages you and lifts up your spirit When I used to travel and sing, I noticed how people are encouraged by songs that encourage worship.

A church I worked with had these three words posted in a place everyone would see: Belong, Believe, Become. These words, especially the first one, encouraged so many people who came to the church for the first time. These words were in this order deliberately. People today want to belong. They want to come to a place they feel community.

> "They drew a line that shut me out,
> Heretic, rebel, a thing to flout!
> But love and I had the wit to win
> We drew a circle and brought them in"[54]

⚜ ENCOURAGING ONE ANOTHER PERSUADES BELIEVERS TO CONTINUE IN THE FAITH

Believers are not to see through one another. They are to see one another through. This is being significant.

During an ice storm in 2006, I noticed how beautiful the ice-covered trees looked with the sun shining on them. I also noticed the trees had less damage when the trees were together. Where a tree stood alone, there was tremendous damage, with limbs of the tree broken off.

The lesson for believers is that strength and safety are found when they are together. The state motto of Kentucky is clear: United we stand. Divided we fall.

My friends in the ministry encourage me to keep on course and to keep the ministry God has called me to. In my heart, I know I am not alone.

In your church, you are not alone. You come together to worship the Lord and for encouragement to be faithful.

⚜ ENCOURAGING ONE ANOTHER SUPPORTS YOU IN THE STRUGGLE

"But exhort one another daily, while it is called "Today," lest any of you be hardened through the deceitfulness of sin" (Heb

3:13, NKJV). When we exhort or encourage one other, we find strength for the day. I tell people that they need to pat people on the shoulder, because every time someone gets kicked in the rear, they need ten people to pat them on the back. People are living in discouraging times and when you speak encouragement into their lives you give them the courage to face the day and hope for a better day.

Paul reminds the believers in Thessalonica that he had sent Timothy "to establish you and encourage you concerning your faith, that no one should be shaken by these afflictions ..." (1 Thes 3:2–3). Think about a time when you were encouraged and how the person encouraged you. It may have been a single word or some simple action like opening a door that encouraged you. How can you replicate this for others?

▲ ENCOURAGING ONE ANOTHER IMPARTS LIFE

"There is one who speaks like the piercings of a sword, but the tongue of the wise promotes health" (Prov 12:18, NKJV).

I remember a time a woman in our church was in the hospital for an extended period. I would visit here every few days and pray with her. Every time I left her room I would look back and say, "You're gonna make it." One time I came she looked at me and said, "I'm mad at you." I asked her why. "The last time you left you didn't say, 'You're gonna make it.'" You never know how a few words will encourage someone or how the lack of a few words will discourage someone. For the rest of the time she was in the hospital, I left with these words, "You're gonna make it!"

"Death and life are in the power of the tongue, and those who love it will eat its fruit" (Prov 18:21, NKJV).

"Let no corrupt word proceed out of your mouth, but what is good for necessary edification, that it may impart grace to the hearers" (Eph 4:29, NKJV).

The people you come in contact with day after day need encouragement. Some people can live on encouragement from another for a longer period, but most people need more encouragement, much like the woman in the hospital. Who can you pat on the back today? Who can you invigorate with an encouraging word or action?

A Reminder From Nature

One year I planted a small oak tree in our backyard in late fall. It looked dead by the time summer came. I decided to dig it up and transplant another in its place but noticed a couple of leaves growing from the lower trunk of the tree. Investigating, I found the small tree had another sign of life. Its stems bent and were not brittle. I decided to give the tree another chance and see what it is like in the fall.

It can be easy sometimes to give up on people. Either they show no signs of being interested in Jesus or they are new believers who show no signs of growing. When I think of my own life, I am filled with joy as I realize God did not give up on me. As you realize God's grace in your life, you must extend it to others. God is not giving up on you. He has already sent others to you who will not give up either.

Who can you come alongside today to encourage?

Remember Barnabas? His name means "son of encouragement." He was definitely an encouragement to Saul (Paul). "And when Saul had come to Jerusalem, he tried to join the disciples; but they were all afraid of him, and did not believe that he was a disciple. 27 But Barnabas took him and brought him to the apostles. And he declared to them how he had seen the Lord on the road, and that He had spoken to him, and how he had preached boldly at Damascus in the name of Jesus" (Acts 9:26–27). Barnabas believed in people and acted on that belief by helping them. He got involved with people. To encourage others, you must get involved.

The Milestone of Significance Is Achieved When We become Intentional.

Now let's get practical. What can you do to encourage others?

- send a card
- make a phone call
- pat someone on the shoulder
- visit someone
- go sit with someone
- cry with someone
- pray with someone
- share Scripture with someone
- tell someone not to give up and remind the person others are standing with him or her
- tell someone, "You are going to make it"

Restore someone by bringing that person back on course. Be part of the Christian community the Lord has designed.

▲ Reflection

Who can you encourage today?

Who can you add value to today?

Who can you make a difference for today?

Who has encouraged you today?

Take to heart the instruction found in 1 Thessalonians 5:11, "Therefore comfort each other and edify one another, just as you also are doing" (NKJV).

If you find self is getting in your way, becoming a roadblock, it can be overcome!

If you find fear a roadblock, it can be overcome!

If you find stress a roadblock, it can be overcome!

If you find the lack of self-confidence or insecurity a roadblock, it can be overcome!

If you find lack of purpose a roadblock, it can be overcome!

If you find unhealthy relationships a roadblock, it can be overcome!

If you find frustration a roadblock, it can be overcome!

If you find powerlessness a roadblock, it can be overcome!

When you find others who have come against roadblocks, help them overcome!

One Last Thought

Who energizes you? Those who energize me are those who encourage or add value.

Think about a time this past week you experienced someone encouraging you. Who challenged you to be a better person and energized you.

Think about your conversations with people yesterday. Who gave you energy? Who drained you? What made the difference? What characteristics do you admire in those who energize you?

Reflect on your conversations with people the last couple of days. Who did you energize? Who left my conversation drained?

Be intentional in your efforts to encourage or add value to someone today. You may find the people you add value to or encourage today will add value or encourage you tomorrow.

Keep walking in the journey of significance and you will make a difference in the lives of others daily. "Therefore, my beloved brothers, be steadfast, immovable, always abounding in the work of the Lord, knowing that in the Lord your labor is not in vain" (1 Cor 15:58).

Endnotes

1 John Maxwell, *How to Influence People* (Nashvile, Thomas Nelson, 2013), 6.

2 John Maxwell, *Intentional Living* (New York: Center Street Hachette Book Group, 2015), 4.

3 Nelson Mandala, *From Freedom to the Future: Tributes and Speeches* (South Africa: Jonathan Ball, 2003), 480. http://db.nelsonmandela. org/speeches/pub_view.asp?pg=item&ItemID=NMS708, Used with Permission.

4 Hal Heydon, Ed., *The Gigantic Book of Running Quotations* (New York: The Skyhorses Publishing, Inc., 2003), 85.

5 Booker T. Washington. 1907. *Up From Slavery: An Autobiography.* New York: Doubleday, Page & Co.. 39. https://www.google.com/ books/edition/Up_From_Slavery/xN45ZsUMgKEC?hl=en&gbpv= 1&dq=up+from+slavery&printsec=frontcover

6 Earl Jabay, *The Kingdom of Self, A Fresh Penetrating Analysis Of Your Greatest Predicament* (Plainfield, New Jersey: Logos International., 1974), 11.

7 Source, *Protagoras by Plato*, Project Gutenberg, Translated by Benjamin Jowett, (Kindle Location 64).

8 Kenyon, E. W., *What Happened from the Cross to the Throne* (Kenyon's Gospel Pub Co., 1946), 111.

9 Brenda Euland, *"Tell me More"* (Article) Ladies' Home Journal (Philadelphia, Pennsylvania: Curtis Publishing Company, November, 1941), 51.

10 Stephen R. Covey *The Seven Habits of Highly Effective People* (New York: Free Press, 2004), 239.

11 "Don't Get Caught Making this Big One-on-One Meeting Mistake", *INC Magazine*, April 18, 2019, https://www.inc.com/ford-transit-connect/tip-of-the-day/avoid-this-big-one-on-one-meeting-mistake. html

12 Watchman Nee, *The Normal Christian Life* (Fort Washington, Pennsylvania: CLC Publications, 1977), 27.

13 Paul Negril, *Great Short Poems* (New York, Dover Thrift Editions), 108 [Kindle Edition].

14 F. B. Meyer, *Joshua: and the land of promise* (Fort Washington, Pennsylvania: CLC Publications, 2013), 22.

15 Tal Ben-Shahar. *Chose the Life you Want* (New York: The Experiment llc, Publisher), 66.

16 C. S. Lewis, *The Screwtape Letters* (San francisco: Harper One, 2011), 161. *The Screwtape Letters* by CS Lewis © copyright CS Lewis Pte Ltd 1942. Used with Permision.

17 E. Stanley Jones, *Abundant Living* (Nashville: Abingdon Cooksbury, 1942), 83.

18 John Maxwell, *Man in the Mirror* (John Maxwell.com Blog), October 1, 2014, www.johnmaxwell.com/blog/man-in-the-mirror/

19 The Imperials. *I'm Forgiven* (Word, 1979), Track 2, One More Song For You.

20 Corrrie Ten Boom, *Clippings from My Notebook* (Nashville, Thomas Nelson, 1982), 19.

21 Dan Meyer, "Hung up: How Do I Forgive Myself?", April 2012, Preaching Today, https://preachingtoday.com/sermons/sermons/2012/april/hunguphowforgive

22 Helen Holwarth Lemmel, *"Turn Your Eyes Upon Jesus"* (Sing His Praise, Springfield, Missiouri, Gospel Publishing House, 1991), 329..

23 The Imperials. *I'm Forgiven.*

24 Anne S. Murphy, *"Constantly Abiding" (Sing His Praise, Springfield, Missiouri, Gospel Publishing House, 1991),131.*

25 M.M.H. *"Be Still"*, published 1919, https://hymnary.org/hymn/VLH1919 /95

26 S. Jaysbee, *The Iron Man of India* (R. P. Bookwala, 1951), 57. https://www.google.com/books/edition/The_Iron_Man_of_India/LbxOAAAAMAAJ?hl=en

27 Edward Demarkus, Ed., *The Ultimate Book of Quotations* (Charleston, South Carolina: Create Space), 394.

28 W. E. Cornell, *"Wonderful Peace"* (Sing His Praise, Springfield, Missiouri, Gospel Publishing House, 1991), 157.

29 Merrill Unger. The New Unger's Bible Dictionary Chicago: Moody Press, 1957. WORDsearch CROSS e-book.

30 Laurence Richards, *New International Encylcopedia of Bible Words* (Zondervan, 1991), 6.

31 Dan Reiland, The Pastor's Coach (Blog), danreiland.com. Used with Permission.

32 Abrahan Joshua Herschel, *A Passion for Truth* (Farrar, Straus and Giroux, 2011) [Kindle Location 2039]

33 Ralph J. Cudworth, *A Treatise Concerning Eternal and Immutable Morality*, edited by Sara Hutton (Cambridge University Press, 1996), 131.

34 Selwyn Duke. 2009. Stopping truth at the border: banning Michael Savage from Britain (Article). 2009. https://www.renewamerica.com/columns/duke/090506

35 Bruce   Howell.   2007.   https://www.sermoncentral.com/sermon-illustrations/63299/on-stories-by-bruce-howell,

36 Daren Polk, Better Life Coaching (Blog). 2012. https://betterlifecoachingblog.com/2012/01/06/the-eagle-and-the-chickens-a-story-about-being-who-you-are-meant-to-be/

37 Greg White, *Vision and Mission Statement*, 2013. https://www.cantonillinois.org/vertical/sites/%7B3A712A47-3D50-49B4-9E78-DBB8A8D0F159%7D/uploads/Vision and Mission Statement for website.pdf

38 Alice Gray, *Stories from the Heart* (Multnomah Publications, 2001), 116.

39 James F. Engle., Wilbert Norton, *What's Gone Wrong With the World? A Communication Strategy for the Church and World Eveangelism* (Grand Rapids, Michigan: Academie Books, 1975), 45.

40 Jillette Pen, *A Gift of a Bible, Pen Says (Blog)* http://www.crackle.com/c/penn-says/a-gift-of-a-bible/2415037", (Penn Says episode 192, 2008), Crackle, 2:59

41 R. T. Kendall, *The Anointing* (Thomas Nelson, 1998) [Kindle Locations 717-719].

42 C. S. Lewis, *Letters to Malcolm: Chiefly on Prayer* (Harper Collins, 2017), 75. *Letters to Malcolm* by CS Lewis © copyright CS Lewis Pte Ltd 1963, 1963. Used with permission.

43 Lawrence Stone, *The Story of the Bible*, www.storyofbible.com/the-one-who-falls-down-beside-us.html (Accessed March 8, 2021).

44 R. A, Torrey, *Why God Used D. L. Moody* (Article), *https://wholesomewords.org/biography/biomoody6.html*

45 Assembly of God, *Fundamental Truths*, 7, Baptism into the Holy Spirit, https://ag.org/beliefs/statement-of-fundamental-truths#7

46 R. A.Torrey, *The Holy Spirit* (New York, Fleming H. Revell Company, 1927), 109.

47 R. A.Torrey, *The Holy Spirit* (New York, Fleming H. Revell Company, 1927), 112.

48 R. A.Torrey, *The Holy Spirit* (New York, Fleming H. Revell Company, 1927), 117.

49 Edward Geil, Evangelist, *A Modern Parable. The Factory That Would Not Go* (*The Railway Signal*, February 1903) p. 31, https://www.google.com/books/edition/Railway_Signal/TCs2AAAAIAAJ?hl=en

50 Bill Easum, *Dancing with Dinosaurs* (Nashville: Abington Press, 1993), Back Cover of Book.

51 Fred Smith, *Leadership Journal on Christian Humility*; http://www.ctlibrary.com/le/1984/winter/84l1118.html

52 John Maxwell, Tim Elmore, Executive Editors, *Maxwell Leadership Bible NKJV* (Thomas Nelson, 2007), 1347. (reworded to match this books chapters).

53 Leonardo Da Vinci, *Notebooks,* Edited and Introduction by Emma Dickens (Simon & Schuster, 2005), 113.

54 Edward Markham, Outwitted, *Shoes of Happiness* (Doubleday, Page and Company, 1915), 2.

About the Author

Greg graduated from Central Bible College (Now Evangel University) with a degree in Bible. He struggled early with what to preach and how to find his own voice. He found encouragement while taking a graduate level course on Expository Preaching with the late Dr. Warren Wiersbe. This course made a difference in his life and continues to inspire him to pass on what he has learned. Greg was an associate pastor for 2 years and pastored for 38 years in churches from 25 in attendance to 300. Along the journey he worked through unique challenges that come with pastoring churches of varying sizes.

Greg served in his district as Men's Representative, Section Alternate Presbyter and Presbyter. He served as Chairman of the Red Cross in Ford County, and President of the Ministerial Association in most towns he pastored. He was asked to serve on the board of Directors at Canton Chamber of Commerce, while there he chaired the business and community committee. Greg joined the John Maxwell Team, March 2012.

Greg loves to encourage people and especially people in ministry and helping pastors and church leaders to grow and navigate roadblocks which make them stuck. Encouraging and training leaders energizes them to grow and make a difference in their calling and career.

Lightning Source UK Ltd.
Milton Keynes UK
UKHW020633200521
384056UK00013B/656